KT-560-503

FROM
RY

OF
ER

KA 0108880 7

THE CENTURION OF CAMULODUNUM
(No. 7)

By kind permission of the Colchester and Essex Museum

Frontispiece

THE ROMANS IN BRITAIN

AN ANTHOLOGY OF INSCRIPTIONS

With Translations and a Running Commentary

By A. R. BURN

Reader in Ancient History
in the University of Glasgow

OXFORD
BASIL BLACKWELL
M·CM·LXIX

© *Basil Blackwell* 1969

631 11400 9

*Library of Congress Catalog
Card No.*: 68-28310

First printed 1932
Second edition 1969

KING ALFRED'S COLLEGE
WINCHESTER

942·013
BUR   25371

Printed by Robert Cunningham and Sons Ltd, Alva
and bound by the Kemp Hall Bindery, Oxford

TO THE MEMORY OF
MY MOTHER
WHO FIRST INTRODUCED ME
TO HADRIAN'S WALL

CONTENTS

CONTENTS

LIST OF PLATES

PREFACE TO THE SECOND EDITION

The demand for a reissue of the modest introduction to Romano-British inscriptions, which I wrote when teaching the Sixth Form at Uppingham in 1930-1, is gratifying, but has for some years been an embarrassment. I could not tolerate a mere reprint; the text contained far too many errors, as was pointed out by R. G. Collingwood in a kindly and encouraging review; new discoveries, many of them important, continued to multiply; and other work has hitherto prevented me from undertaking the extensive rewriting and numerous additions necessary. The present edition has been made possible by the appearance of *The Roman Inscriptions of Britain*, Vol. 1, containing all the inscriptions on stone (and some on other materials) discovered up to the end of 1954, which enormously facilitated the work of checking and correcting; also by the invaluable assistance of my recent pupil, Mr A. B. Watson, who undertook the retyping of the whole book, including the insertion of my new material from loose sheets, the transposition of a number of items, renumbering and the insertion of cross-references; a task calculated to defeat any secretary who was not a scholar, and some scholars too. My warm thanks are due to him, and to Mr R. P. Wright, the sole editor of *RIB* since the death of Collingwood in 1943, who generously encouraged me to proceed with this edition, rather than to await any Select Inscriptions of his own after the completion of his work on *RIB*, Vol. II (inscriptions and *graffiti* on pottery and other *instrumentum domesticum*).

I have introduced in this edition references to 'sources', i.e. to authoritative publications. Numbers standing alone opposite the bottom, left corner of a text refer to *RIB* I; numbers prefixed by 'CIL' to the *Corpus Inscriptionum Latinarum*; by 'D' to Dessau's *Inscr. Lat. Selectae*; 'AE' to *L'Année Épigraphique*, and 'JRS' to Mr Wright's annual publication of new finds from Britain in the Journal of Roman Studies. *BM* = British Museum (*Guide to the Antiquities of Roman Britain*, 1922).

A. R. BURN

Glasgow, 1967

INTRODUCTION

On Roman Inscriptions

The greatest achievement of Rome was the organisation of the Roman Empire—not Roman literature, but the Roman peace, although Rome's greatest historian permits his British highlander to remark that it was often the peace of a depopulated country. It follows that Rome's greatest work was done in the provinces, not at home; and accordingly the modern study of Roman imperial history turns away from the sensational but squalid topic of the enormities of Caligula and Nero to look at Roman methods of administration, and the daily lives of ordinary folk throughout the vast Empire and in the army that protected it.

Here, however, the ancient historians fail us rather badly. It is characteristic of the intellectual sterility of the Empire that throughout its whole extent and through all the four centuries for which it survived in the west, only one first-class historian appears; and even Tacitus is great not as a historian, but as a rhetorician, a phrasemaker, and a satirist in disguise. His bad are much more interesting than his good characters; he is not in the least interested in the manners and customs of peoples within and without the Empire, unless they are in some way piquant and bizarre; he divides his text about equally between unsatisfactory accounts of wars on the frontiers, together with such other more sensational events as earthquakes and the prosecutions of corrupt or oppressive provincial governors, and a highly-coloured but depressing history of the Palatine backstairs.

It is the archaeologist who gives us the information for which we look in vain to the ancient historians. The realistic school of Roman sculpture, for instance, shows us the butcher, the baker, the leather-goods maker, at work in their shops. Photographs from Trajan's Column are the obvious source of illustrations to any work on the Roman army. It is these, much more than the literature, that enable us to picture to ourselves the men and women who walked the streets of Rome, Pompeii and Timgad, Verulamium and Silchester: the men who built the amphitheatres and aqueducts of Italy and Provence and, nearer home, planned the Roman roads of Britain and the course of Hadrian's Wall. And of these material remains none is more important than the inscriptions. To quote the father of modern Romano-British studies[1]:

'The inhabitants of the Roman Empire filled their cemeteries with elaborate monuments, and frequently inscribed upon them not only the name and the virtues of those buried below, but their ages, birthplaces, professions, and careers. In their temples they erected altars to their gods, and carved on these altars the titles both of the gods and of themselves. In their cities they recorded similarly, not only the completion of their chief public buildings, but the services of their chief citizens, . . . and even important decrees passed by their town councils. In their fortresses they equally placed on permanent record the dates when various buildings were first finished or repaired, the officers concerned with the works, the troops then in garrison and many such details. The result is that Roman inscriptions contain a vast amount of incidental information about the history of the Roman Empire. Single inscriptions rarely reveal much, but when many are taken together they tell us a great deal of which we should otherwise be ignorant. . . . The ancient historians tell us very little about the Roman Empire. We turn to the inscriptions. From them we learn a vast variety of facts. We learn for instance the names and careers of the officers commanding various troops and the governors who control the provinces. We learn the series of promotions by which a man rose to a military command or a provincial governorship, and what social rank was necessary for success in aiming at such posts. We learn whence the common soldiers were levied, how long they served, what kind of promotion was open to them, what bounty or reward they received on retirement, and even the fortunes which attended them in the rest of their lives. We can trace the gradual diffusion of the Roman franchise through the provinces, the gradual disappearance of the old native names and languages, and the increase of civilised town life.' Even in the outlying and thinly-populated province of Britain, well over 2,000 inscriptions have been found; and 'they

[1] Haverfield; Introduction to his Catalogue of Roman inscriptions in the Carlisle Museum.

tell us where the forts and fortresses were, what were their garrisons, whence the troops were recruited—and what was the whole system of frontier defence against the Caledonians, along the line of the great Wall and of the roads leading up to it'.

Such is the scientific interest of these inscriptions. They have also a sentimental interest. What may be called the relic-hunting instinct in man is irrational, no doubt, but not on that account the less deep-seated; and it does seem to increase the vividness of our impression of a bygone age, to reflect that we are reading here not the imaginative reconstructions of a historian, but the actual words with which this or that Roman soldier dedicated his altar to Unconquered Mithras, or the old Italian God of the Wild Woods, or the Spirit of the British Countryside; or, in other contexts, the words which Paternus the Briton, away in Germany, chose for the tombstone of his 'fellow-soldier and best friend'; or Marcellinus, at Corbridge on the Tyne, for that of his little girl; or Aurelius Marcus 'of the century of Obsequens' for that of Aurelia 'his sainted wife, who lived for thirty-three years without stain'.

In the first edition I attempted to give a complete list of all auxiliary regiments known for the Hadrianic period. The list now given (see No. 100 and Index II) is longer, but does *not* attempt to be complete. Readers wishing to engage in the fascinating study of the *auxilia* of the Roman Army must be referred to Professor H. Nesselhauf's full publication of the 'diplomas' in *CIL* XVI and its Supplements I and II, and for Britain to *RIB* (including the diplomas from Britain in Vol. II, forthcoming); also to Professor E. B. Birley's important articles in *JRS*, 1932, and in *Transactions of the Cumberland and Westmorland Archaeological Society*, 1939; and look out for new discoveries in *JRS* and *AE*.

CHAPTER I

THE CONQUEST
(A.D. 43-85)

This chapter covers the period of Romano-British history of which our literary sources tell us most, since we have accounts of the campaigns of Ostorius, Suetonius, and Agricola, from the pen of Tacitus, as well as the author's brief allusions, in his *Agricola*, to other governors. Inscriptions on the other hand are less numerous for this than for the second or third centuries. Consequently in this chapter the inscriptions do not form our main source, as in the other sections, but rather serve to illustrate and amplify a narrative derived mainly from Tacitus. Yet even here they supply, as we shall see, some valuable details of geographical and economic information of the kind that the great historian, with his limited outlook, here as usual ignores.

§1   THE FIRST TWENTY YEARS

A MONUMENT AT ROME

1)   TI · CLAV[dio · Drusi · f · Cai]SARI
         AVGV[sto · Germani]CO
      PONTIFIC [i · maximo · trib · potes] TATXI
      COS · V · IM[p – – – patri   ·   pa]TRIAI
      SENATVS · PO [pulusque.] RO [manus·q]VOD
      REGES · BRIT[anniai] · XI [devictos · sine
      VLLA · IACTVR[a · in · deditionem · acceperit
      GENTESQVE · B[arbaras · trans · Oceanum · sitas
      PRIMVS·INDICI [onem · populi · Romani · redegerit
CIL VI, 920
D 216

'To Tiberius Claudius, son of Drusus, Caesar Augustus Germanicus, High Priest of the State, in the eleventh year of his holding the tribunician power, five times consul, · · · times saluted "Imperator", Father of his Country, the Senate and People of Rome (dedicate this arch), for that he subdued eleven kings of Britain without any reverse, and received their *surrender, and was the first to bring barbarian nations beyond the Outer Seas under the Roman sway.'*

The inscription is restored out of fragments (indicated by capitals); but all dedications in honour of emperors follow certain well-defined formal lines, so that the gaps (indicated by brackets and small print) can be filled in with some confidence.

The spellings Caisar, patriai, for Caesar, patriae, etc., are archaisms. Claudius was an antiquary, not to say a pedant, and preferred the spelling found in the earliest Latin writers.

Emperors were re-endowed every year with that power as tribune which gave legal sanction to their position in home affairs. *Trib. potestat. XI.* therefore gives us the date, A.D. 51 or 52, eight years after the first invasion of the island; the eleventh year of Claudius' reign, and that of the capture of Caratacus.

Roman generals under the republic were acclaimed as 'Imperator', 'a true General', by their troops in moments of enthusiasm after a victory. Under the Empire, each new emperor, being legally commander-in-chief of the forces, was so acclaimed by the armies at the beginning of his reign, and again after any important victory, by the troops engaged. For troops to salute their own commander as Imperator was an act of high treason; it implied nothing less than the intention to make him emperor.

Claudius, though he left the command of the expeditionary force in the capable hands of Aulus Plautius, had taken part in the campaign to the extent of spending just over a fortnight in Britain, watching the troops go forward to the storm of Colchester, the capital of Caratacus the son of the late king Cymbeline, and personally receiving their salutations afterwards.

A NATIVE PRINCE

2)
         N] EPTVNO   ·   ET   ·   MINERVAE
                      TEMPLVM
         PR] O · SALVTE · DOM [VS] · DIVINAE
         EX ·] AVCTORITA [TE · TI ·] CLAVD ·
         CO] GIDVBNI·R·LEGA [T] ·AVG·IN·BRIT·
         COLLE] GIVM·FABRORVM·ET·QVI·IN·EO
         SVN] T · D · S · D · DONANTE · AREAM
91
         CLEM] ENTE · PVDENTINI · FIL

An inscription from near Chichester, recording the dedication of a temple by friendly natives as a demonstration of loyalty to the Empire:

'*To Neptune and Minerva this temple (is dedicated, with prayers) for the safety of the divine (i.e. the imperial) house, at the desire of Tiberius Claudius Cogidubnus, King and Imperial Governor in Britain, by the Metalworkers' Company and its members, at their own cost, the site being presented by Clemens, son of Pudentinus.*'

R. presumably = *rex*; D.S.D = *de suo dederunt* or *dedicaverunt*.

When Aulus Plautius marched on Colchester through the home counties, the tribe in Sussex, probably called the Bodunni, was left isolated in his rear. Its king, Cogidubnus or -dumnus, threatened of old by the House of Cymbeline, submitted and was rewarded with Roman citizenship and extended territories to rule as an imperial Lord-Lieutenant, 'Legatus Augusti'. The floors of his great Romanising palace at Fishbourne have been among the major discoveries of the 1960s. The whole population of his enlarged kingdom came to be known as the Regnenses, 'People of the Kingdom'. According to Roman custom, the new citizen takes the individual and clan names of the person granting citizenship, in this case the Emperor Claudius himself, while keeping his own personal name as a Roman *cognomen*. The temple probably dates from some years after Plautius' campaign.

The Metalworkers' Guild was no doubt rich and important; Cogidubnus' kingdom included the great iron-working district of the Weald.

THE LEGIONS IN THE SOUTH AND MIDLANDS

Tacitus tells us the names of the four legions engaged in the conquest of southern Britain, and something of their exploits, but knowing, as he did, very little and caring less about the geography of this barbarous country, he gives us only the roughest ideas as to where they went. Inscriptions help, by giving us a few fixed points.

Tiles for use in roofing the buildings of a legion's permanent or semi-permanent camp were often stamped with the regimental number and titles, in an abbreviated form, as a safeguard against 'scrounging'. Material relics of the conquest of the south and midlands are few; it was swift and final, and the legions moved on to Northumbria and Wales. The evidence even of these humble utensils is therefore not to be despised.

STAMPED TILES

3)   (a) Seaton, Devon: LIIG II AVG
          (b) Bristol: LEG II AVG
          (c) Whittlebury, Northants: LEGXXVV
RIB II   (d) North of Castor, Northants: LEG IX HISP

The letter II, in (a), is a way of writing E, common in the 'running hand' of the time and now and then appearing in inscriptions (cf. No. 20).

From the home counties, then, we find the legions moving out separately fan-wise across the country. It was the best thing to do, for the tribes never attempted to combine. As Tacitus says 'they fight separately and are united in subjection'.

Legion II Augusta, forming, with its auxilia, the left column, was under a capable general of humble birth named Titus Flavius Vespasianus, then (A.D. 45) about thirty-five years old. He had already distinguished himself in the early pitched battle in Kent. Under his command the legion conquered Wessex, capturing the Isle of Wight by an 'amphibious' operation, fighting thirty actions in the field, and taking twenty fortresses[1]—the great entrenchments of the chalk downs among them—and penetrating as far as Devon and the Bristol Channel, as the inscriptions show. Caesar's campaigns in Gaul were on a larger scale, but not more swift and thorough than the work of Vespasian and his little army of some ten thousand men.

On the right, the Ninth Legion, called 'Spanish' for early service in that country, moved through the east midlands, where the tile from Castor, on the Nene, marks its passage; at the other end of the county, two marches to the south-west, the tile bearing the stamp of 'Leg.XX. V. V.'—The Twentieth, Valeria, Victrix—must also date from first-century campaigns. The surname of this legion probably commemorates its service under Augustus' general Valerius Messalinus, in the crisis of A.D. 6-9—the desperate revolt of the newly conquered Danube provinces, which three fifths of the whole imperial army were barely enough to quell.

Finally, the left centre was formed by the afterwards famous

---

[1] These details are given by Suetonius, Life of Vespasian, c. 4.

legion, XIV Gemina; this title, 'Twin', or 'Double', is borne by several legions. It is explained as referring to their creation at some period or other of the Civil Wars, by the fusion of two much-depleted corps.

In A.D. 47, Plautius was recalled to his well-earned 'ovation', and succeeded by Publius Ostorius Scapula. The new governor repulsed an invasion of the conquered territory by the still independent tribes of the west; he humbled the powerful Iceni of the east, when they, at first friendly, resisted disarmament; he superintended the planting of a Roman colony at Camulodunum, whence the modern name Col-(onia)-chester; and according to the most probable reading of a corrupt passage in Tacitus,[1] he consolidated Roman rule up to the line of the Trent and Severn. In his battle with the Iceni, his young son, serving as a subaltern on his father's staff, won the Civic Crown, the 'Victoria Cross of the Roman army', awarded to a soldier of any rank who had saved the life of a comrade in the face of the enemy. After this Ostorius attacked the Decangi or Deceangli of Flint and Cheshire, penetrating nearly to the Irish Sea. Probably in or not long after his time the Ninth Legion was established at Lincoln, the Second at Gloucester, and the Fourteenth at Wroxeter—Uriconium, or Viroconium, the place whose name still survives as that of the neighbouring height, the Wrekin.

THE FOURTEENTH AT WROXETER

4)

```
        M   PETRONIVS
        L  ·  F  ·  MEN
        VIC    ·    ANN
        X X X V I I I
        MIL    ·    LEG
        XIIII   ·   GEM
        M I L I T A V I T
        ANN   ·   XVIII
        SIGN   ·   FVIT
294     H  ·  S  ·  E
```

---

[1] *Annals*, xii, 31; the text reads *cuncta castris antonam et sabrinam fluvios cohibere parat*, of which, as it stands, it is very difficult to make anything like sense. A very neat emendation, now generally accepted, is to read *cuncta cis Trisantonam et Sabrinam*, etc., supposing Trisantona ('Thrice Holy'—a Celtic river-name known elsewhere) to be the name of the Trent.

'*Marcus Petronius, son of Lucius, of the tribe Menenia, from Vicenza, aged 38 years: soldier in Legion XIV, Gemina: He served for eighteen years and was standard-bearer. He lies here.*'

H.S.E. = Hic situs (or sepultus) est; the regular *early* formula.

The tribe Menenia is one of the 35 voting divisions of republican Rome, to one of which every citizen was still assigned under the early empire.

THE NINTH AT LINCOLN

5)

C · SAVFEIO

C·F·FAB·HER

MILITI·LEGIO

VIIII

ANNOR·XXXX

STIP · XXII

255
H · S · E

'*To Gaius Saufeius, son of Gaius, of the tribe Fabia, from Heraclea, Soldier in Legion IX Hispana, who lived for 40 years and served for 22. He lies here.*'

Names, which like this one, have no *cognomen* are usually of early date. By the second century practically everyone has one.

There were numerous Greek cities called Heraclea, but as none but Roman citizens might enlist in the Legions this is probably Heraclea in Macedonia, where a Roman colony had been planted.

6)

C · VALERIVS · C · F

MAEC · MIL · LEG

IX · SIGN · ⟩ HOSPITIS

ANN·XXXV STIP·XIIII

. . . .

257
(Stone broken at bottom.)

'*(Here lies) Gaius Valerius, son of Gaius, of the tribe Maecia, soldier in Legion IX, Standard-bearer of Hospes' Company, who lived for 35 years and served for 14.*'

⟩, an old Etruscan sign for K = Company (*centuria*) *or* Centurion.

A CENTURION OF THE TWENTIETH

Meanwhile the Twentieth, in the early years of the conquest, *may* have had its winter quarters at Camulodunum itself, as a garrison among the Catuvellauni. (It was never, as used to be thought, at Wroxeter *with* the Fourteenth; the camp there is only of a size for one legion.) Whether for this reason or as a member of a smaller guard at the civil capital, or otherwise, there died here a centurion of the Twentieth, whose portrait tombstone, once realistically painted, is one of the finest pieces of classical sculpture in Britain. It is hardly at all weathered, having been broken and thrown down in soft mud, which preserved it, probably when Boudicca sacked Colchester in 61. Near it was a lead urn containing burnt bones, and a cup datable about A.D. 50-60. The centurion stands, bare-headed, but in corselet and kilt, girt with his sword and dagger, and holding in his hand the vine-stick that was the symbol of a centurion's power to flog defaulters. Below is the inscription:

7)   M·FAVON·M·F·POL·FACI
                LIS· ⟩ ·LEG·XX·VERECVND
                VS·ET·NOVICIVS·LIB·POSV
                ERVNT · H · S · E

200   (Frontispiece)

'Marcus Favonius Facilis, son of Marcus, of the tribe Pollia, Centurion in the Twentieth Legion. Verecundus and Novicius his freedmen set this up. He lies here.'

THE AUXILIARY COHORTS

Nor, when praising the legions, should we forget the cohorts and cavalry *alae* of *socii*, recruited among the non-citizen population of the Empire, serving for a minimum of twenty-five years, as against twenty for the legions, and receiving citizenship only on discharge. They supplied half the infantry and almost the entire cavalry of the imperial army; they took their part with the legions on the day of battle, and bore the brunt of the wear and tear of guerilla warfare, communications, raids, reconnaissance and frontier patrols, that the citizen legionaries might be as fresh as possible when the enemy was brought to bay.

Towards the end of Ostorius' command, the war came to a head more and more along the borders of South Wales. For year after year the indefatigable Caratacus, Caradoc the son of Cymbeline, driven from his father's kingdom but still unconquered,

kept the resistance alive there, among the dark and—as Tacitus
says (*Agricola*, c. 11)—Spanish-looking Silures. At last Caratacus,
having encouraged the Ordovices, the northern neighbours of
the Silures, to risk a battle, with disastrous results, found it
prudent to leave their territory; he fled to Cartimandua, queen of
the powerful Brigantes of Northumbria, only to be handed over in
chains to his lifelong enemies. He was sent to Rome, where 'as
every schoolboy knows', his fearless demeanour won him
pardon for his crime of nationalism. He was kept in honourable
captivity, while inscr. 1, above, celebrates Claudius' victory.

All the early tombstones of auxiliaries that we possess are of
cavalrymen, more highly paid, probably of a higher social class in
their home tribes, and more likely to make arrangements in their
wills for such monuments. Here are the inscriptions from two
fine sculptured slabs, each showing a Roman cavalry-soldier
riding down an enemy:

From Cirencester

8)
       DANNICVS · EQES · ALAE
       INDIAN · TVR · ALBANI ·
       STIP · XVI · CIVES · RAVR ·
       CVR · FVLVIVS · NATALIS · ET
       FLAVIVS·BITVCVS·ER·TESTAME·
       H·S·E

108

'*Dannicus, Trooper in Indus' Horse, Albanus' Troop, served 16 years.
He was a citizen of Raurica. Fulvius Natalis and Flavius Bitucus, his
heirs, had this set up according to his will. He lies here.*'

The Ala Indiana was one of nearly a score of Gallic Cavalry
regiments which bear names, apparently derived from personal
names, but no serial numbers. This one was probably named after
Julius Indus, a chief of the Treveri (near Trier), mentioned by
Tacitus[1] as having suppressed a rebellious movement in his tribe in
the reign of Tiberius. The regiment had seen service on the
Rhine before being sent to Britain, and reappears on that frontier
later. Raurica Augusta is the modern Augst, on the upper Rhine,
a great source of soldiers. Albanus, the leader of Dannicus' *turma*

---

[1] *Annals*, iii, 42.

(a troop of 30), chances to bear the name same as the third-century martyr, St. Alban.

STIP. = *stipendium*, = pay, and so a year's pay and so a year's service. CIVES is simply a mistake for *civis*. ER·TESTAME = *heredes, testamento*. It was regular practice for the donor of a tombstone to put his own name on it as well as that of the deceased.

From Gloucester

9)   RVFVS · SITA · EQVES · CHO · VI
      TRACVM · ANN · XL · STIP XXII
      HEREDES·EXS·TEST·F·CVRAVE·
                H·S·E

121

'*Rufus Sita, Trooper in the Sixth Thracian Cohort; in the fortieth year of his age and the twenty-second of his service. His heirs had this set up, according to his will. He lies here.*'

A cohort was an infantry battalion of either 480 or, more rarely, 960 men; but a certain number were *equitatae*, that is to say contained 360 infantry and four *turmae* of mounted men. The arrangement had obvious advantages in frontier warfare in which small detachments of both arms were often wanted.

EXS is another mistake, for EX. Celtic and Thracian cavalrymen were mightier with the sword than with the pen.

The Economic Background

The project of invading Britain had the whole-hearted support of the numerous and influential people at Rome who hoped to make money out of it. These included not only the clever Greek freedmen-secretaries through whom Claudius ruled the Empire, and lesser finance officers, but even such an almost episcopal figure as Seneca, the scholar and Stoic philosopher who was tutor to Nero, the Emperor's young stepson. Among other things, Britain was believed to be rich in gold, silver, and pearls. The actual yield of these proved disappointing, but in the process of silver-mining much lead was found. The export of this must have been enormous; for some scores of Roman 'pigs' of the metal are now known, and these represent only chance finds in modern times of the chance losses of Roman times—losses incurred chiefly in transit, no doubt by pack-animals. They will be published in the forthcoming *RIB* II.

Minerals among the Greeks and Romans were the property of the state, though mines might be leased to private individuals. Consequently most of the pigs, which, like some legionary tiles, are always stamped, bear the name and titles of the reigning emperor. Often they are also dated. The two earliest help to show how very promptly exploitation began:

10)   TI·CLAVD·CAESAR·AVG·P·M·TR·P·VIIII·
                IMP·XVI·DE·BRITAN·

RIB II

'*Tiberius Claudius Caesar Augustus, Pontifex Maximus, nine times endowed with the tribunician power, sixteen times saluted Imperator: From Britain.*'

The date = A.D. 49, and the ingot was found in the Mendip Hills; so mining was already in full swing in the west within six years from the landing of the first Roman soldier.

11)   BRITANNIC·AVG·II
                 V ET P

BM, p.30

The manager who designed this stamp does not seem to have been quite sure about the Emperor's titles; Claudius was of course offered the honorific title of Britannicus after the victories in Britain, but instead of accepting it himself, chose to confer it on his infant son. The letters V ET P, roughly added on one side of the ingot, stand for 'Veranius and Pompeius', the names of the consuls for A.D. 49. This bar also comes from Somerset.

12)   NERONIS AVG EX K IAN IIII COS BRIT
               EX ARGENT CNPASCI

BM, p.29

'*Property of Nero Augustus, Consul from the first of January for the fourth time. British lead from the silver workings of (Gnaeus Pascius?)*'

Found at Stockbridge, Hants; evidently lost in transit to the coast. The date = A.D. 60. The consulship was, under the Empire, held for less than a whole year, in order that this purely honorary distinction, regularly conferred, like a modern peerage, on distinguished soldiers and lawyers, especially those selected to be viceroys of the more important provinces, might be shared by more men. To be consul from the Kalends of January, and so to give one's name to the year, was more honourable than to hold the office later.

With these may be quoted three tiles:

13)   NER CL CAEAVG GER
RIB II

'*Nero Claudius Caesar Augustus Germanicus.*'

Printed with a wooden stamp while the clay was still soft; highly abbreviated, with several ligatured letters—Æ, A/, ɛR. From Silchester, a small country town but a tribal capital, Calleva of the Atrebates. Of interest as showing that besides mines, the Emperor had other property—perhaps that of some dispossessed British chief—in the territory conquered by Vespasian.

14)   (*a*)   P ·PR · BR
           (*b*)   P·P·BRI·LON

BM, p.26

From London. No evidence as to the date; they *may* be as early as Nero's reign. The stamps stand for (*a*) '*Publicans of the Province of Britain*' and (*b*) '*Publicans of the Province of Britain, London.*'

Roman government was anything but a blessing to Britain in the first twenty years. Tacitus himself makes the Britons inveigh bitterly against the extortion of swindling traders, tax-farmers, and usurers, who could usually rely on government support against the natives. Another grievance, to which the province was to grow used in time, was the conscription of young men who were deported to the equivalent of twenty-five years' hard labour in auxiliary cohorts on the Rhine or Danube. There is extant a military diploma (on these, see below, Nos 95, 100) of A.D. 84, from the Danube frontier, recording the grant of Roman citizenship to time-expired auxiliaries, which if it were not too long might be quoted here; for one of the cohorts named is called 'I Britannica'—and since in 84 some of its men had completed twenty-five years' service, we have evidence that it was levied not later than 59.

Ostorius Scapula died in harness in the year 52, worn out by the long guerilla warfare against the Silures. This tribe struck back again and again against the Romans, not infrequently with success. They trapped and destroyed two cohorts of auxiliaries in the summer following the capture of Caratacus; and before the arrival of Aulus Didius, Ostorius' successor, they even defeated a legion under one Manlius Valens. Didius, an old man, drove them back into their hills but did little more; and his successor Veranius, consul in 49 (cf. No. 11), died within a year of his arrival. But then came once more a great soldier, Suetonius Paullinus, who determined to strike at the root of British national feeling by the extirpation of Druidism. With the Fourteenth and Twentieth Legions and their auxilia, he reached the isle of Anglesey and destroyed its sacred groves. On his staff there served a young officer whom we shall meet again, Gnaeus Julius Agricola.

In that same summer of 61, the philosopher Seneca, requiring some ready money, suddenly called in his vast loans in Britain. He had probably been indulging in a popular Roman method of money-making—that of lending to provincials, at high rates of interest, the ready money that they had to have to pay the taxes. Doubtless he knew nothing of the human side of these trans-actions; whether that makes his conduct worse need not be discussed here. Many Britons were feeling the anger of despair; the governor and the main body of his army were far away; and the spark that fired the magazine was supplied by the treatment of Queen Boudicca of the Iceni.

The story is well known, how King Prasutagus, when dying, left half his property to the emperor, in the hope that Rome might be satisfied and allow his wife and daughters to possess the other half; how the officers and soldiers sent to take possession looted his house like that of a conquered enemy and grievously maltreated the widow and orphans; how the Iceni, Trinovantes, and Catuvellauni rose as one man under Boudicca's leadership, and attacked the Roman officials and traders everywhere, sacking the colony of Camulodunum and killing every Roman man, woman and child whom they caught.

The Ninth Legion, the only considerable Roman force in the east of the island, was under a gallant and impetuous officer named Petillius Cerialis. He came swiftly to the rescue, was met by superior numbers, and suffered a disaster which crippled his legion and sent him back with the remnants to his fortified base. This was the news that met Suetonius, who hurried back to London at the first news of the revolt.

Suetonius found the large, open town untenable. Some days behind him were his infantry: the Fourteenth Legion and a detachment of the Twentieth, the rest of which had to be left to overawe North Wales. Horsemen had long since been despatched to Paenius Postumus, a quartermaster-general in acting command of the Second, bidding him march eastward; but Postumus lost his nerve and cowered inactive. Suetonius was forced to make a terrible retreat; those civilians who could march with the army, did so; but women, children and old people fell behind and were killed without mercy by the pursuing Britons. To have waited for them would not have saved them; to fight anywhere but in a position with its flanks covered would only have involved the Fourteenth Legion in the fate of the Ninth.

Not till he reached such a position did Paullinus halt. Then, on a rising ground, with flanks and rear covered by forest, he stood at bay. The Britons pressed on in confident and disorderly array; the Roman javelins took heavy toll of their dense masses; then, at Suetonius' order, the whole line rushed forward. The enemy wavered and broke, but their own numbers and their huge wagon-train hindered their flight. The Roman sword and the lances of the cavalry continued the slaughter until weariness and nightfall ended it; the back of the rebellion was broken. The Fourteenth Legion had covered itself with glory, and received the additional titles of Martia, Victrix, for this day's work.

Boudicca took poison; Postumus of the Second fell on his sword rather than face the chief he had disobeyed; and Suetonius took revenge on the rebellious tribes with merciless severity; but Julius Classicianus, the new Procurator (chief finance officer), replacing one who had done much by his greed and cruelty to cause the rebellion, reported to Rome that the reprisals were positively deterring rebels from laying down their arms. The financial service was not under the military governors, but reported directly to the Emperor; a system which, if it often caused friction, had been none the less agreeable on that account to the wily Augustus, as making it more difficult for military chiefs to plan rebellion. One of the Emperor's chief secretaries, a Greek freedman, was sent out to report; and, to the great indignation of the young Agricola (echoed by Tacitus), Suetonius was superseded.

JULIUS CLASSICIANUS

Classicianus died on service, and was buried in London; and two large stones from his tomb, re-used centuries later in the Roman city wall, shed an interesting light on his family background:

15)

D I S

M] A N I B V S

C·IVL·C·F·F]AB·ALPINI·CLASSICIANI

*   *   *   *

PROC·PROVINC·BRIT[ANNIAE]

IVLIA·INDI·FILIA·PACATA·I[ndiana ?]

VXOR [F ?]

12

'*To the Divine Shades of Gaius Julius Alpinus Classicianus, son of Gaius, of the tribe Fabia . . . , Procurator of the Province of Britain. Julia Pacata, daughter of Indus, . . . his wife (set this up).*'

Dis Manibus (cf. No. 21, etc.) was a phrase then just coming into vogue.

Two lines, which would have recorded Classicianus' earlier career, were on a block unfortunately still missing—probably not far underground, in the city of London—somewhere. But it is the identity of his wife, 'Indus' Daughter', as she proudly reminds us, that is illuminating. Indus, Julius Indus, a great enough man to be so mentioned without possibility of ambiguity, must have been that chief of the Gallic Treveri whom we have already mentioned (No. 8 note); 'Indus of Indus' Horse'. The man who counselled mercy to Celtic rebels was himself married into a Celtic aristocracy.

It does not follow that Classicianus was himself a Trever; he could have been from Italy. Roman officials did marry chieftains' daughters. But the fact that the names Alpinus and Classicus both occur among the Treveri makes it quite likely. If so, it is a good example of the spread of Romanisation. A Greek and a Gaul put an end to reprisals after the bloodiest episode in the Roman conquest of Britain.

The government had had a fright. For seven years there were no more adventures in the north and west of Britain, and in 68 Nero withdrew the now famous Fourteenth Legion to swell his army for a projected war of conquest in the east; and then followed A.D. 69, the year of Four Emperors, when, after the murder of Nero, the Guards at Rome and the armies of the Rhine and the East (the last supported by the Danube legions) fought each to place their own nominee on the imperial throne.

A Veteran of the British Wars

16) *M. Vettio M. F. Ani. Valenti, mil. coh. viii pr. benef. praef. pr., donis donato bello Britan. torquibus armillis phaleris, evoc. Aug. corona aurea donat.,* > *coh. vi vig.,* > *stat.,* > *coh. xvi urb.,* > *coh. ii pr., exercitatori equit. speculatorum, princip. praetori leg. xiii. Gem, (p. p.) (?) ex trec. leg. vi Victr., donis donato ob res prospere gest. contra Astures, torq. phaler. arm., trib. coh. v vig., trib. coh. xii urb., trib. coh. iii pr., [trib.] (?) leg. xiiii Gem. mart. victr., proc. Imp. Caes. Aug. prov. Lusitan., patron. coloniae, speculator. x. h. c., L. Luccio Telesino, C. Suetonio Paulino cos.*

D 2648

At Rimini (Ariminum); an honorary inscription, recording the career of an officer risen from the ranks of the Praetorian Guard.

The sign > is the regular abbreviation of *centuria* or *centurio*.

'To Marcus Vettius Valens, son of Marcus, of the tribe Aniensis, Soldier of the Eighth Cohort of the Guard, attached to the staff of the Commandant of the Guard, decorated in the British War with neck-chains, medals and armlets, decorated as a re-enlisted veteran in the Imperial Forces with a golden crown, Centurion in the Sixth Cohort of the Watch, Centurion of Dispatch Runners, Centurion in the Sixteenth Urban Cohort, Centurion in the Second Cohort of the Guard, Riding Instructor of the Mounted Police, Headquarters Centurion of Legion XIII Gemina, Leading Centurion after being Trecenarius, in Legion VI Victrix, decorated for successes against the Asturians with neck-chains, medals and armlets, Tribune of the Fifth Cohort of the Watch, Tribune of the Twelfth Urban Cohort, Tribune of the Third Cohort of the Guard, Tribune (?) in Legion XIV Gemina Martia Victrix, Imperial Procurator of the Province of Lusitania, Patron of this Colony, the Ten Military

Police Constables of the Colony (erect this) to do him honour, in the Consulship of Lucius Telesinus and Gaius Suetonius Paulinus.'

The date is A.D. 66. Suetonius, though relieved of his command because his severity was thought to be prolonging the war, is honoured for his victories with a second consulship.

Valens' service in Britain while a guardsman is evidence that Claudius employed part of this ornamental and highly-paid division on the campaign—doubtless among the reinforcements which joined Plautius' army with the Emperor himself. These Praetorian Cohorts, each 1,000 strong, were under Augustus nine in number, afterwards twelve and then again only ten. After them the three Urban Cohorts at Rome were numbered straight on—X, XI, XII, under Augustus—but enjoyed less prestige; their business was to preserve order in the city, not the life and person of the Princeps. A Thirteenth Urban Cohort was stationed at Lyons; the Sixteenth, in which Valens serves as a centurion, is no doubt this one; XVI when the numbers were raised.

Much inferior in prestige were the seven cohorts of *Vigiles*, recruited from the despised freedman class, barracked at various points divided among the fourteen Regions of the City, and functioning as a semi-military police and fire-brigade.

The *torques phalerae armillae* with which Valens is decorated in Britain were the regular decorations for private soldiers and non-commissioned officers up to the rank of centurion. They were conferred all together. They were made of some bright metal of little intrinsic value, and were worn on ceremonial parades.

After serving his time (sixteen years, for a guardsman) Valens rejoins the colours as an *evocatus Augusti*. Such re-enlisted veterans were much valued, and after receiving for some service unspecified the high distinction of the golden circlet, which could be worn on the helmet—a decoration usually reserved for senior centurions—Valens sets foot on the ladder of promotion. The *statores Augusti*, among whom he serves as a centurion, were the Emperor's orderlies. After successive promotions as centurion among the troops at Rome, he reaches the responsible post of *princeps praetori*, in Legion XIII in Pannonia; this post was held by the second in seniority of the legion's sixty centurions, and from its title seems to be that of a kind of sergeant-major of the divisional staff. In his next promotion, Mommsen believed that he became *primus pilus*, Leading Centurion, the title in its abbreviated form *p.p.* having dropped out, before *ex trecenario*; such minor errors are quite common in inscriptions. This would certainly be logical promotion. The *primus pilus* was regularly summoned to councils of war, with the young commissioned officers, the Tribunes of the Soldiers; and as neither these young gentlemen nor sometimes the *legatus legionis* himself had nearly as much military experience as their grim and grizzled warrant-officers, both *primus pilus* and *princeps praetori* must often have been in positions of the utmost responsibility, and, in matters of routine and tactics at least, have really 'run' the Legion. The term *trecenarius* has not been satisfactorily explained; it is applied, however, to senior centurions in the Guards, and since it can hardly refer to salary (the figure is too high) it may, as Mommsen thought, mean 'commanding 300 men'.

Decorated once more for suppressing a revolt of the Asturians, Valens now reaches the rank of tribune, attained by very few ex-privates. Once more he works through the various grades of the city soldiery, and is finally seconded again to a legion. This promotion takes him back once more to Britain; his legion is the now famous Fourteenth Gemina Martia Victrix. The last two of these titles never appear before this date, and in later centuries are often abbreviated; but now, only five years after the great battle with Boudicca, they are proudly flaunted in full. Martia is of course the adjective from Mars—as one might say, the 'fighting Fourteenth'.

Having next served as *procurator* in Portugal—a post which in a small province meant 'governor', in a large one like Lusitania the chief finance officer, reporting directly to the Emperor—we leave Valens, something over fifty years of age, to look back on a successful and varied career, and to contemplate a present in which he has attained the rank of a Roman knight and is an important enough personage to be in demand as a 'patron' of the new colony at Ariminum, and the recipient of an honorary inscription from the ten military policemen on the governor's staff (*h.c.* = *honoris causa*). Later inscriptions from Rimini show that his family flourished there and reached the ranks of the Roman Senate. One of them (2nd century?) was even 'retained' by the notables of Britain to look after their interests as Patron of

the Province in which his ancestor had once served as a plain
guardsman.

§2   VESPASIAN'S THREE GENERALS

Vespasian, the old commander of the Second Legion, after getting
into serious trouble and being dismissed the court for going to
sleep when Nero was giving a musical performance, was un-
expectedly summoned from his retirement in 67 and placed in
command of the army that was to suppress a serious rebellion in
Judaea. Nero, who dreaded the rebellion of some too successful
general, felt that Vespasian was safe, as his low birth made him
'impossible' as a candidate for the purple. However, the impossible
happened, and in 69 Vespasian actually was pushed rather
unwillingly by the eastern armies and his colleague, the Governor
of Syria, into proclaiming himself Emperor. Among the first
to declare for him when the Danube legions invaded Italy on his
behalf were two ex-officers of the British wars—Quintus Petillius
Cerialis, who was a cousin of his, and in Provence Julius Agricola.
Cerialis commanded a cavalry column in the final advance on
Rome and once more advanced impetuously and suffered a
rebuff.

Vespasian is rather faintly praised by some historians. The fact
is that Roman gossip, represented for us by Suetonius Tranquillus'
biography, never quite forgave him for not being a gentleman.
He remained to his death a Sabine farmer, who called a *plaustrum*
a *plostrum*,[1] cared much for efficiency and economy but not a rap
for etiquette, and had a keen if indelicate sense of humour. But he
remains one of the very greatest Roman Emperors. He ended the
Jewish War, which was not of his making; he rounded off the
province of Britain, which his predecessors had left with unsatisfactory frontiers; he inaugurated in Germany the system of
frontier defence that culminates with Hadrian's Wall in Britain;
and above all, by rigid economy, yet without stinting either the
army or educational expenditure, he restored the imperial
finances, which after Nero's extravagance, followed by two civil
wars and two serious rebellions, showed a deficit equivalent to
a thousand million top day-wages.

[1] Florus the littérateur once ventured to tell him so, only to be loudly greeted in
public the following day 'Good morning Flaurus'.

His first appointment to the governorship of Britain was that of Cerialis, who in 70 had crushed a rebellion among the Gallic and German native regiments on the Rhine. With him, now a *legatus* in command of a legion, served Agricola.

Tacitus as usual gives us little exact information as to the strength and movements of the army; but from this point inscriptions begin to give a really considerable amount of information.

A tombstone at Wroxeter may show the Twentieth replacing the Fourteenth Legion there for a time:

17)

C · MANNIVS
C·F·POL·SECV
NDVS·POLLEN
MIL LEG · XX
ANORV · LII ·
STIP · XXXI
BEN·LEG·PR·
H·S·E

293

'*Gaius Mannius Secundus, son of Gaius, of the tribe Pollia, from Pollentia, Soldier in Legion XX, aged 52, and having served for 31 years; a member of the staff of the Commandant. He lies here.*'

The second N of *annus* is quite often omitted in inscriptions.

BEN·LEG· = *beneficiarius legati*, 'a member of the staff of the legate'. The Romans never quite got out of the way of regarding appointment to a desirable and responsible position as a 'favour', a *beneficium*, to be conferred on one's own acquaintances or friends.

PR. possibly = *praetorii*—the legate of praetorian rank in command of the legion as opposed to the legate, an ex-consul, in command of the whole province and army.

The Twentieth was Agricola's legion. Detachments from the British legions had fought alongside the Rhine army against Vespasian, in the desperate night battle near Cremona, that decided the civil war, and Agricola found his men still inclined to be slack and insubordinate. He dealt with them by tact rather than severity, and the legion's achievements in the next few years show his success.

R.B.—C

A New Legion

To send a governor like Cerialis to a province like Britain clearly foreshadowed a 'forward policy', and Vespasian took care to provide adequate forces. Tacitus tells us vaguely that the army was increased. These stones (among others) show us what the new troops were, and where they were stationed. Three tombstones of men of a new legion have been found at Lincoln; available as winter quarters for this not yet veteran information, for reasons which will appear.

Two of the emperors of 69 had raised each a legion from among the sailors of the fleet. Vespasian now takes them into the regular army, with the numbers and title I and II Adiutrix—literally 'Assistant', a name no doubt intended to be honourable while also marking the originally irregular character of the regiments; for the Roman navy was very definitely a junior service and its sailors were recruited from among non-citizens. The Second Adiutrix has also acquired the titles Pia, Fidelis, 'Loyal and True', at some crisis of the civil war. It is this which now appears in Britain:

18)   Above: a trident between two dolphins

> T·VALERIVS·T·F
> CLA·PUDENS·SAV
> MIL·LEG·II·A·P·F·
> 〉 DOSSENNI
> PROCVLI · A · XXX
> AFRAN·HE·D·S·P
> H·S·E

Below: an entrenching-tool
(Lincoln)
258 (with slightly different reading of l. 6)

'Here lies Titus Valerius Pudens, son of Titus, of the tribe Claudia, from Savaria, Soldier in Legion II A.P.F., Dossennius Proculus' Company, aged 30. Afranius his heir (set this up) at his own cost.'

Claudia Savaria is now Szombathely in Hungary. Claudius planted there a Roman colony, all members of which belonged to the tribe Claudia.

The reading of the last line but one is uncertain; the stone is slightly damaged. D.S.P. however = *de sua pecunia*, or *de sua posuit*. The stone, which is in the British Museum, is an attractive one. The trident between dolphins, above, alludes to Valerius' service across the sea; the pioneer's axe, to the ordinary routine of a legionary's life in peace-time.

THE ADVANCE TO YORK

Along the Pennine chain and beyond, from Derbyshire to Dumfriesshire, stretched the territory of the Brigantes, the most powerful of all the British tribes. Cartimandua, the Queen who surrendered Caratacus, had a consort named Venutius, an ally of Rome since the days of Claudius, but later she came to prefer his armour-bearer (who would also be a Celtic nobleman), and the tribesmen, deeply suspicious of Rome, rallied round the injured husband; the queen had the support of the Romans. They had kept her in power for some time, but in the bad days of 69, Venutius won. A Roman force rescued the queen but could do no more than retreat with her into Roman territory. Rome's Brigantian policy was in ruins and had to be restored; so Cerialis paid his old legionaries the compliment of giving them some of the hardest fighting in the division's chequered career. As a result, the base-camp was moved forward from Lincoln to York, close to the centre of the tribe's power. Cerialis penetrated indeed much farther north; but his temperament favoured attack rather than consolidation; the dalesmen gave blow for blow; and there is doubtless truth, as well as a tendency to contrast Cerialis with Tacitus' own hero, Agricola, in the historian's summary—'the whole territory of the tribe was conquered, or at least invaded'.

A TILE FROM ALDBOROUGH

19)
RIB II

LEG VIIII HISP

Aldborough, twenty miles north-west of York, close to the confluence of the Ure and Swale, was in those days Isurium Brigantum, very probably the Celtic capital. The legion's presence there will date probably from before the foundation of the fortress at Eburacum.

The Base at York

A Soldier's Dedication:

20)

```
       D [E O              S A N C T O
       S I L V A [N O         ·        S
       L    ·    C E L E R I N [I] V S
       V I T A L I S      ·      C O R N I
       L E G   ·   VIIII   ·   H I S
       V  ·  S  ·  L  ·  L  ·  M
       FIDO   NVMINI   HOC   DONVM
       ADPIIRTINEAT CAVTVM ATTIGGAM
```

659

'To the holy god Silvanus, Lucius Celerinius Vitalis, Clerk in Legion IX Hispana, pays his vow gladly willingly and duly. Let this gift be a possession for the faithful god. I must not touch it.'

Roughly cut, and quaintly phrased and spelt. (*Attiggam* for *attingam*.) II = E; cf. No. 3(a). s = *sacrum*.

CORNI = *Cornicularius*. Vitalis is evidently an orderly-room clerk on the staff of the *legatus* of the legion. V S L L M = *Votum solvit laetus libens merito*, a formula repeatedly found in inscriptions recording dedicatory offerings, both in full and abbreviated, with small variations.

Silvanus, the old Italian Spirit of the Wild Woods, became a favourite god of the soldiers, as they marched and camped in unknown lands. He receives the epithets *Castrensis*, Spirit of the Camp, and *Invictus*, like the soldiers' god Mithras; and dedications to him are numerous in Britain.

The Pacification of Wales

Cerialis' successor was a man in the strongest possible contrast to him, Sextus Julius Frontinus, an engineer and a theoretical soldier, the author of a book *De Re Militari*, both on military routine in peace-time and on the art of war. It is unfortunately lost, but a notebook of his—a collection of 'Stratagems'—still exists, as well as a technical treatise on the aqueducts that supplied Rome with water.

With his engineer's instinct to make sure of his foundations, the new governor declined to press on in the north before making an end in Wales, and his great work was the subjugation of the Silures. To his time belongs the forward move of the Second (Augusta) Legion to Isca Silurum, still called in Welsh 'Fortress of the Legion', Caerleon, on the Usk—nor has the neighbouring river changed its name. It was a well-chosen site, lying between the tribal capital at Caerwent, Venta Silurum, a short march to the eastward, and the hills in which the real strength of the Silures lay.

ISCA OF THE SILURES

21)

```
D               ·               M
G  ·  VALERIVS  ·  G  ·  F
GALERIA         ·      VICTOR
LVGDVNI · SIG · LEG · II · AVG
STIP · XVII · ANNOR · XLV · CV
RA·AGINTE·ANNIO·PERPETVO·H
```

365

'*Sacred to the memory of Gaius Valerius Victor, son of Gaius, of the tribe Galeria, born at Lugdunum, Standard-bearer in Legion II Augusta, served for 17 years and lived for 45. (This stone was set up) under the superintendence of Annius Perpetuus his heir.*'

D.M. = Dis Manibus (literally 'To the Divine Departed'; cf. no. 15) gradually becomes the regular formula on tombstones, replacing the earlier H.S.E.

Lugdunum—presumably the most famous of the cities of that name, Lyons. *Cura aginte = curam agente.*

The letters are cut larger at the top than at the bottom of the stone; hence the greater number of letters in the lower lines. The finely cut letters and the phraseology suggest an early date.

Among the remains of the legionary fortress, tiles with the legend

22)   LEG II AVG

RIB II

are naturally numerous.

THE AUXILIARIES IN WALES

Meanwhile the auxiliary cohorts, scattered among the dozen fortified outposts, at such strategically important points as river-

crossings and the heads of the mountain valleys, with which
Frontinus secured the land of the Silures, bore the burden of
preserving the Roman peace. Inscribed stones are rare in these
forts, which were only fully garrisoned for a generation or two
while the Silures were learning to keep the peace; and all probably
really date rather later, when earth and timber forts were being replaced in stone. Later still, we find most auxilia concentrated in
the north. Here, however, are a few fragments of Roman stone
from far north-west of Caerleon, later built into farm-buildings at
Llanio-isaf (*a* and *c*) and of the Church at Llan-ddewi Brefi:

23)   (*a*)   COH·II·ASTVR
407   *'Second Asturian Cohort'*

           (*b*)   .... MIBVS ...
                  [COH·I]I ASTV (R ...
                  'To the ...
408   *Second Astur(ian Cohort)'*

           (*c*)   Ɔ VERIONI
                  'Verionius' Company.'
411

Roman forts, like Roman roads, were built by the very skilful
labour, chiefly of the legionaries. They took a pride in their work
and liked to perpetuate the memory of it. Hence dozens of
elaborate or rough inscriptions in which sometimes a legion,
much more often a cohort or century will record its completion
of a building or a gateway or so many yards of wall.

The methodical advance of the Legion up the valley of the Usk
is also suggested by two tiles with the legend:

24)   LEG II AVG
RIB II

One of these is a day's march up the river from Isca, at
Gobannium, whose name survives in Abergavenny; the other,
thirty miles further north and west, close to the headwaters of the
river, at the fort called Y Gaer, near Brecknock, in the heart of the
hills.

MORE ECONOMICS

Inscription on a pig of lead in the British Museum, found on Hints Common, Staffordshire:

25)   On top: IMP·VESP·VII·T·IMP·V·COS
                Scratched on side: DECEANGL.

BM, pp. 29ff

'*Imperator Vespasian for the seventh time, Titus, Imperator, for the fifth time, consuls. (From the country of the) Deceangli.*'

The date is A.D. 76. The Deceangli seem to have lived in Flint and Cheshire (Tac., *Annals*, xii, 32). So mining was already in full swing there, even before North Wales was completely conquered.

Both Vespasian himself and his eldest son and fellow-consul for this year are *imperatores*; but the Emperor, following a precedent first set by Julius Caesar, puts the title first, as though it were part of his name, while Titus, like a general under the republic, has it only as a title.

A similar pig, but without the letters scratched on the side, lost, like this one, in transit on Hints Common, is in Tamworth Castle.

THE CONQUEST OF NORTH WALES

Meanwhile Julius Agricola, who had distinguished himself repeatedly in the campaigns of Cerialis, had been recalled to further honours at Rome. He had served for a space as governor of Aquitaine, and been raised to the consulship. In 78 he returned once more to Britain as commander-in-chief. His first campaign was against the Ordovices of Snowdonia, who had successfully cut up a cavalry *ala* just before his arrival. He brought them to battle and made a terrible slaughter of them; after which he subdued Anglesey, which he had last seen as a young subaltern in the year of Boudicca's rebellion, seventeen years before. It is amusing to see how both Cerialis and Agricola as commanders-in-chief return at the first opportunity to the scenes of their old campaigns.

26)   A FORT IN NORTH WALES

    (*a*) Ɔ PERPETVI   (*b*) Ɔ PERPE

427 P XXII   TVI

                              425 ·P·XX

    (*c*) Ɔ IVL   (*d*) Ɔ IVLI

       P E R P E T V I   PERPETVI

423 ·P·X X I   424 PXXXIX

          (*e*) Ɔ P E R P E

         426 P X X I

'*Century of Julius Perpetuus; 39 feet (of wall).*'
(Etcetera.)

    P. = either *passus* or *pedes.*

Five building-inscriptions from the later rebuilding in stone of one of the forts with which Snowdonia and the rest of the Ordovician country was now secured. They are now in the Segontium Museum, Caernarvon. The fort is on the southern borders of the Ordovices at Tomen-y-mur, where the road goes over the hills from Festiniog to Dolgelly.

AGRICOLA AT CHESTER

Agricola or Frontinus also brought over Legion II, Adiutrix, from Lincoln to the strategic point of Chester. A silver denarius in mint condition, lost between two stones in the walls during construction, dates the building of the legionary fortress here precisely to the seventies; and piped water was being laid on in Agricola's first year as governor, as is shown by a dated inscription on a lead pipe:

27)   IMP·VESP·VIIII·T·IMP·VII·COS·CN·IVLIO·

              AGRICOLA·LEG·AVG·PR·PR

RIB II

'*In the ninth consulship of the Emperor Vespasian and the seventh of Titus, Imperator, under Gnaeus Julius Agricola, His Majesty's Lieutenant Governor.*'

    LEG·AVG·PR·PR = *Legatus Augusti pro praetore*, 'Lieutenant of His Majesty ranking as propraetor', the regular title of first-class provincial governors in provinces ruled by the Emperor. Such governors in the greater provinces were regularly, like Agricola, of consular rank; but in constitutional theory the real proconsul of such a province was the Emperor, in virtue of the proconsular *imperium* over more than half the Empire (including all the great military frontiers) conferred on him by the senate under Augustus' constitution. So, if the emperor was the legal governor, the *legatus* or lieutenant-governor whom he deputes to govern a province for him must be one step lower in rank—theoretically a propraetor. The title of proconsul *is* used, on the contrary, by the governors of provinces, often of much less importance, who held their commands directly from the senate and not through the Emperor.

Thanks to the fact that he married his daughter to Tacitus, who afterwards wrote a short memoir of him (containing, by the way, precisely seven British place-, river-, or mountain-names) we know Agricola as a man better than any other governor of Roman Britain. It is typical of the fragmentary nature of our evidence that but for this chance we should have heard of him only through a short paragraph of Dio Cassius, mostly wrong, and two inscriptions: this and No. 40.

LEGION II ADIUTRIX AT CHESTER

Excavation has shown that Chester was a normal sized fortress for one legion, and can never, as used to be thought, have contained two at once. Leg.II Adiutrix, which left Britain about 85-86, must therefore have been its first garrison. Several tombstones commemorate its presence.

28)   (Broken at top)

. . . .
ESIS · PVDENS · C · FIL
SER · AVGVSTA · EQ
VES · LEG · II · AD · P · F
ANNORVM · XXXII
S T I P E N D I O R V M
XIII · H · S · ES[T]
(At Chester)

482

'Here lies ———esis Pudens, son of Gaius, of the tribe Sergia, from Augusta, Trooper in Legion II Adiutrix Pia Fidelis, who lived for 32 years and served for thirteen.'

Augusta was the name of numerous cities of the Roman Empire; the dead man's comrades do not tell us which this is.

Under Julius Caesar a legion consisted solely of five or six thousand infantry, but under the Empire it was found useful to attach to it four *turmae* of horsemen as orderlies, and for scouting and advance-guard work.

29)   (Broken at top)

. . . .
II·AD·P·F· ⟩ PETΛONI
FIDI   ·   STIPENDIO
ΛVM · XI · ANNOΛ
VM·XXV
HIC · SEP · EST
(Chester)

481

'Here lies buried —— of Legion II Ad. P. F., Petronius Fidus' Company, who served for eleven years and lived for 25.'

The letter Λ or λ was a way of writing R, common in cursive writing with pen or stilus; it is surprising to meet on a stone inscription. Cf. however II for E in Nos 20, 3(a).

Haverfield thought there must be a mistake in the stone's assertion that the soldier enlisted as a boy of fourteen; but the legion was raised during the excitement of the Civil Wars; and 'such things have been'.

THE AUXILIA IN LANCASHIRE

Two tiles:

30)   (a)   COH III BR
                       (b)   COH III BR [A?]

RIB II

'Third Bracarian Cohort.' (Cf. Nos. 95, 100.)

The tiles are from two positions successively occupied by the same regiment, from Bracara Augusta, near Lisbon, probably during Agricola's operations in the north-west of England. (a) is from the Roman fort at Manchester, (b), which is broken off short, from that at Castleshaw, bleakly situated on the high moors of the Lancashire and Yorkshire border.

A LEGION-COMMANDER

A group of inscriptions from Antioch in Pisidia, north of the Taurus, shows us the rise of a family, one of whose members became Agricola's right-hand man holding down the newly-conquered Brigantes while Agricola was finishing off in Wales. An engineer-officer under Augustus, C. Caristanius Fronto (the family name is a rare one) was a leading man in a *colonia* of veterans which Augustus settled at Antioch, and acting-mayor when the famous Quirinius, Governor of Syria, was elected Honorary Mayor. His grandson (?), with the same names, was in 69 commanding a regiment of native cavalry from the Crimea, serving on the Euphrates; it later appears on the Danube, having probably marched to Europe in the campaign that made Vespasian emperor. Having served the Flavian cause, Caristanius was promoted to the Senate in Grade II from the bottom without the formality of holding the junior senatorial offices, and then to Grade III (praetorian) to make him available for important commands; a colonel becoming a general as the direct result of a revolution.

31)

```
          C · C A R I S [T A
  N I O · C · F · S E R · F [R O N
  TONI · TRIB · MIL · P [RAEF ·
  EQ · AL · BOSP · ADL [E
  CTO · IN · SENATV · INTE [R
  TRIBVNIC · PROMOTO · IN
  TER · PRAETORIOS · LEG · PRO
  PR·PONTI·ET·BITHYN·LEG·IMP
  DIVI · VESPASIANI · AVG · LEG
  IX · HISPANAE · IN · BRITANN
  LEG · PROPR · DIVI · TITI
  CAES·AVG·ET·IMP·DOMITIAN
  CAES · AVG · PROVINC · PAM
  PHYLIAE · ET · LYCIAE · PATRO
          N O · C O L
  T · C A R I S T A N I V S · C A L
  P V R N I A N V S · R V F V S
  OB · MERITA · EIVS · HC
```

See G. L. Cheesman in *JRS* III (1913).

'*To Gaius Caristanius Fronto, son of Gaius, of the Tribe Sergia, military tribune; commander of the Bosporan Cavalry Regiment: enrolled in the senate in the Tribunician rank; promoted to Praetorian rank: Imperial Governor of Pontus and Bithynia; General Officer of His late Majesty Vespasianus Augustus, commanding Legion IX Hispana in Britain; Imperial Governor of His late Majesty Titus Caesar Augustus and His Majesty Domitianus Augustus, of the Province of Pamphylia and Lycia; Patron of this Colony; Titus Caristanius Calpurnianus in recognition of his service set up this monument.*'

H.C. = *hoc curavit.*

Caristanius holds three successive praetorian posts; they were usually held for about three years each. His legion-command, sandwiched between two provincial governorships, both in his native Asia Minor, will have fallen under Frontinus and in Agricola's first year. He later reached the consulship in A.D. 90. We shall meet with another member of the Antioch branch of the family later (No. 128).

MORE LEAD MINES

32)
RIB II   IMP·CAES·DOMITIANO·AVG·COS·VII

'*In the seventh consulship of the Emperor Domitianus Caesar Augustus.*'

A pig of lead of the usual type, from Hayshaw Moor in the West Riding, dated A.D. 81. The vultures follow the eagles with their usual promptitude. A plentiful supply of slaves to be worked to death in the mines was no doubt provided by Agricola's prisoners of war.[1] To sell the prisoners into slavery was the usual practice in campaigns against barbarians.

AGRICOLA'S TRACK INTO SCOTLAND

On a tile of the usual type from Carlisle:

33)   [LE]G VIIII.
RIB II

On a building-stone of the earliest Roman fort at Camelon, near Falkirk:

[1] Cf. Tac. *Agricola*, 31.3.

34) XXVVF.
2210

The syllable LEG no doubt appeared on the next stone, which has not been found. This will be part of a building-record of the usual type:

'*The Twentieth Legion Valeria Victrix Built this.*'

Both must belong to the Flavian period; the Ninth Legion disappeared from Britain before Hadrian's Wall was built, and No. 34 was found in a smaller fort whose foundations underlie those of the larger second-century post.

Before his recall Agricola had, as is well known, conquered all Britain up to the Highland line, and probably reached the Moray Firth. He advanced methodically, consolidating his gains by the construction of roads and small carefully-sited and very heavily entrenched cohort-forts. One of his roads was the Stanegate, giving lateral communication from the Solway to the Tyne. Tacitus boasts that no fort sited by Agricola had ever (down to the time of writing, about A.D. 100) been either evacuated in the face of the enemy or taken by storm. He probably intends a comparison with Cerialis to the latter's disadvantage; but the history of the next century shows that he was fortunate to be able to advance as he did without suffering a disaster from a rising of the Brigantes in his rear; and he probably owed his immunity to the hammering which they received from Cerialis ten years before.

In 83 he settled a legion at Inchtuthil on the Tay—the northern-most of all Roman legionary fortresses, now meticulously excavated by the late Sir Ian Richmond. By elimination, since we know where his other three legionary headquarters were, it was his own veteran Twentieth. But Inchtuthil, occupied only for a very few years, has yielded no inscriptions.

In the following summer, after an arduous campaign, he also defeated the Caledonians of the Highlands, somewhere far to the north, at Mons Craupius (of which Grampius is a miscopying); perhaps Knock Hill, near the Pass of Grange. Tacitus claims that he was confronted by 30,000 highlanders and killed 10,000; both figures are wildly exaggerated. The warrior strength of all the clans united was estimated by good authorities at no more than

30,000, as lately as the eighteenth century. The Romans had probably the advantage in numbers, as well as in arms, training and equipment.

THE NINTH LEGION IN A.D. 83

Agricola's legions however were not all at full strength. Before this his 'crowning mercy', Tacitus tells of a well planned counter-move by the enemy, while the army was conducting a 'sweep' in several columns. The Ninth Legion was surprised in bivouac by night, its entrenchments rushed, and the legion only just able to save itself by fierce fighting until Agricola came to the rescue. This legion, says Tacitus, was singled out for attack because it was the weakest. An inscription found at Tibur in Italy explains why:

35)   *L. Roscio M. f. Qui. Aeliano Maecio Celeri, cos., procos. provinc. Africae, pr., tr. pl., quaest. Aug., X vir stlitib. iudic., trib. mil. leg. IX Hispan. vexillarior. eiusdem in expeditione Germanica, donato ab imp. Aug. militarib. donis corona vallari et murali, vexillis argenteis II, hastis puris II, salio, C. Vecilius C. f. Pal. Probus amico optimo. L.d.s.c.*
D 1025

An honorary inscription recording the career of a distinguished senator who in his youth was one of Agricola's subalterns.

'To Lucius Roscius Aelianus Maecius Celer, son of Marcus, of the tribe Quirina; Consul, Proconsul of Africa, Praetor, Tribune, Quaestor of the Emperor, Petty Judicial Magistrate, Military Tribune in Legion IX Hispana, and also of a Detachment of that Legion in the German Campaign; honoured by the Emperor with the Military Decorations of the Vallar and Mural crowns, Two Silver Standards, and Two Silver Spears; Member of the Chapter of the Salii. Gaius Vecilius Probus, son of Gaius, of the tribe Palatina, set up this monument to his good friend. Site given by decree of the senate.'

Roscius' offices are given in the order; consulship; other civil positions in order of importance, naturally the opposite order to that in which they were held; military service; and finally, a priesthood.

The Emperor on whom he attends as Quaestor is not named; it was therefore probably Domitian, the tyrant, whose name, after he had been officially damned, is regularly omitted from documents. It is again omitted in the reference to Roscius' military decorations. Domitian had evidently ordered Agricola to detach troops for a campaign of his own on the Rhine.

X vir stlitib. iudic.—The *decemviri stlitibus iudicandis* decided petty law-suits at Rome; this was one of the minor magistracies, with one of which a young man destined for the senatorial *cursus honorum* started his official career. *Stlis* is the archaic and technical word for a law-suit; *lis*, 'strife', is the same word, pruned down in ordinary conversation.

The Mural Crown had originally been the decoration given to the first Roman soldier to scale an enemy's wall; the equivalent *Corona Vallaris* to the first man over or through a stockade; but they had become stereotyped at this time, and are regularly awarded in accordance not with services but with rank. Tribunes and Prefects of equestrian rank receive a crown, silver spearhead (*hasta pura*), and small silver standard (*vexillum*); tribunes of senatorial rank, two of each; *legati* of praetorian rank, three, and ex-consuls four, or enough to decorate a fair-sized dining room.

Salii—the famous and ancient chapter of 'Dancing Priests'.

L.d.s.c. = *locus datus senatus consulto.*

A BRITISH SOLDIER

It is rare for us to know more than the name of any of the humbler people of the Roman Empire; but a discharge-certificate (one of a class of documents, of which we shall have more to say in Chapter III) enables us to reconstruct an outline of the career of one British private in the Roman army, recruited under Agricola, and very likely in one of the British battalions which marched with him to Mons Craupius. Agricola did what he could to fill the gaps in his order of battle, caused by Domitian's command that he should send troops to the Rhine, by putting in line British battalions recruited among southern tribes of 'high fighting quality and proven loyalty', as Tacitus tells us (*Agricola*, 29); such tribes, we guess, as the Dobunni of the Cotswolds and the Cornovii of Shropshire, who, long threatened by the Catuvellauni and natural enemies of the Welsh mountaineers, never fought the Romans as far as we know. After Agricola's recall, all these regiments were transferred to the Danube frontier. It was general imperial policy, since the rebellion in the Rhine in 69-70, not to employ native troops in their home countries. We hear no more of any

British cohorts in Britain except, in the very late service address-list called the *Notitia Dignitatum*, of a solitary cohort of Cornovii, unmentioned in any known inscription.

So it is from the Danube that we have the discharge-certificate, with grant of Roman citizenship and retrospective recognition of his hitherto unofficial marriage, of Lucco, from Gloucestershire. After the usual text of the imperial proclamation and list of the units to which it is addressed, with which we are not here concerned, come the names of the recipient and his family:

36)   COHORT. I BRITANNICAE M. C.R. CVI PRAEST
                   Q. CAECILIVS REDDITVS
                         PEDITI
              LVCCONI TRENI F. DOBVNN.
        ET TVTVLAE BREVCI FILIAE OVXORI EIVS AZAL.
        ET SIMILI   F.   EIVS
        ET LVCCAE FILIAE EIVS
        ET PACATAE FILIAE EIVS

CIL XVI, 49

'*First British Cohort, 1000 Strong, Roman Citizens; Commandant
             Q. Caecilius Redditus.
                 To Private
          Lucco, son of Trenus, Dobunnian;
   and to Tutula, daughter of Breucus, his wife, Azalian;
        and to Similis his son,
        and to Lucca his daughter,
        and to Pacata his daughter.*'

M., C.R., = *milliaria, Civium Romanorum.*

The Azali, Lucco's wife's tribe, were a people of western Hungary, who themselves provided many good soldiers for Rome's Pannonian cohorts. The certificate is dated the 12th January 105 of our era; and Lucco had served for at least twenty-five-years.

So we can restore his biography:

He was born about A.D. 60 in a country occupied, indeed—there was a legion at Gloucester—but little scarred by war, and grew up while the Romans were trying to improve their public relations, after the revolt of Boudicca. He joined the army (probably as a conscript) in 79-80, and suffered with his fellow-

tribesmen the hard transition from the cheerful untidiness of a
Celtic farm to the 'square world' of the Roman camps, under the
lash of the centurion's tongue and stick. He probably marched to
Scotland under Agricola; but by 85 his regiment appears in
Pannonia (Hungary west of the Danube). There they will have
served in Domitian's Dacian Wars, and there Lucco took up with
a local girl, Tutula of the Azali. The army still legally observed
the fiction that serving soldiers had no love-life (cf. 2 *Timothy*,
ii, 4); but in practice it tolerated the presence of the men's
women and children outside the lines. It must have been difficult
to bring up a family on an auxiliary private's pay; probably
Tutula cultivated a patch of land, Lucco helping when he could.
He called his surviving son (most babies in the Roman empire
died) Similis, 'Like' (his father); quite a common name, and a
delicate compliment to his wife's fidelity; his elder daughter
Lucca, after himself.

The regiment distinguished itself in Trajan's first Dacian War,
101-2, when he conquered Transylvania with its gold-mines,
along with several other British regiments, and won the award of
the title, 'Roman Citizens'. It may have carried some increase in
pay; though discipline was still enforced by the centurion's stick,
as it was even in the legions. It was perhaps during the peace
which followed that Lucco called his youngest daughter Pacata,
Pacified.

But the peace did not last. Dacia rebelled, and Lucco's
regiment, just when he was coming due for his honourable
discharge, was marched away down the Danube road to Moesia.
And to regiments in that province his discharge-certificate is
addressed; for Trajan, a soldier who loved his army, took the
generous step of releasing all veterans who were due for discharge,
before the campaign.

Lucco, after twenty years away from Britain, did not return.
He settled, with his discharge gratuity, in Pannonia, near his
wife's people; and so his precious bronze tablet, recording his
status, was found there: Marcus Ulpius Lucco, a Roman citizen.

THE FLAVIAN OCCUPATION IN SCOTLAND

Meanwhile Agricola left southern and eastern Scotland strongly
held. Inscriptions are few to vanishing point; but one rough

tombstone bears signs of being early, probably belonging to the Flavian rather than the Antonine occupation. It is from Ardoch in Strath Allan, probably one of the several places in Roman Britain bearing the river-name Alauna.

37)   DIS · MANIBVS
                             AMMONIVS DA
                             MIONIS Ɔ COH
                             I HISPANORVM
                             STIPENDIORVM
                             XXVII HEREDES
                                  F·C

2213

'*To the Divine Shades. (Here lies) Ammonius, son of Damio, Centurion in the First Spanish Cohort, of 27 years' service. His heirs had this made.*'

Signs of probably first-century date are the writing of *Dis Manibus* in full (it was soon regularly abbreviated to D.M.) and the fact that this centurion, even in an auxiliary unit, is not a Roman citizen (he has no Roman family name). His name Ammonius, indeed, looks eastern.

ROMAN SHIPPING IN THE IRISH SEA

A tombstone from Chester, broken at the top:

38)   . . . .
                       OPTONIS · AD ·SPEM
                       ORDINIS · ⟩ LVCILI
                       INGENVI   ·   QVI
                       NAVFRAGIO · PERIT
                            [H]·S·E

544

'—— *lies* ——, *Under-Officer marked for promotion, of Lucilius Ingenuus' Company, who perished by shipwreck.*'

OPTONIS—i.e., OPTIONIS; the letter omitted was no doubt painted in. The *optio ad spem ordinis* was presumably marked for promotion when a vacancy occurred.

ORDINIS = 'class', 'rank',—i.e. the rank of centurion.

The letter H of 'H·S·E' is omitted for some unknown reason; possibly as Haverfield suggests, it was to have been inserted when the body was actually buried.

The operations of the Roman Irish Sea Squadron are an interesting and almost forgotten episode in history. It is clear that Agricola had great hopes in this quarter. Not only did his fleet do some genuine exploring work, confirming that Britain was an island and 'sighting Thule'—the Shetland Mainland— but he also hoped to use it to conquer Ireland, which he hoped, with a fine optimism, could be subdued by one legion and its average complement of auxiliaries, and believed, with an equally fine vagueness about geography, would prove a useful base against the refractory tribes of northern Spain. To the history of this squadron too belongs the romantic story, with its grim background of human misery, of the Voyage of the Usipi (Tac., *Agricola*, c. 28).

The Usipi dwelt on the Rhine, where the Roman frontier was being tentatively pushed forward. To weaken them in case of revolt, and incidentally strengthen the army elsewhere, five hundred young tribesmen were enrolled as a cohort and shipped over to Britain. There, somewhere on the west coast, they were deposited, very raw material, to be knocked into shape by some veterans and a centurion. This continued until the brutality of a Roman training goaded them to desperation; anyone familiar with Tacitus' account of the complaints of the mutineers of the Rhine and Danube legions in the first book of the *Annals* will sympathise.

One morning some ships of the Irish Sea fleet put in; and the Germans suddenly broke into mutiny, massacred their taskmasters, seized the ships and three pilots, and set out to sail home round the north of Scotland. They had no skill in seamanship; they mistrusted their pressed pilots, and finally killed them. They had to fight the natives of the coast before they could replenish their stock of food—often they had none. Many died; the remainder survived by cannibalism. Yet a remnant actually did round Cape Wrath, cross the North Sea, and reach the German coast; where the natives, being by no means predisposed to be kindly towards castaway Rhinelanders in Roman uniform, promptly captured them and sold them as slaves. And so, in the course of traffic, some of them did finally reach the banks of the Rhine, to be sold to the Romans; 'and so their story became known', concludes Tacitus; but whether the unfortunate wretches then suffered the penalty for desertion, he does not say.

CHAPTER II

THE PROVINCE

§1   BRITAIN SETTLES DOWN

BUILDINGS AT BATH

On a fragment of stone from a monument or the gable of a temple, at Bath:

39)   VES VII CO
172

'—*Vespasian, Consul for the seventh time*—'

The date is A.D. 76. Tacitus tells us much of how Agricola by his personal tact and charm and by the use of every kind of 'moral suasion' won over the chiefs and upper classes among the Britons to take part in Romanisation—coveting and prizing Roman citizenship, wearing the toga with pride, hiring lecturers to give their sons a Roman education, and adorning their towns with Roman municipal buildings and temples to Roman gods in the Roman style. One may doubt whether this wholesale adoption by the conquered of an alien civilisation was altogether healthy or natural[1]; Tacitus himself sneers at it; but to spread a uniform Latin culture over the whole of the West was the aim of the government, and as we shall see from many inscriptions in this chapter it was very successful.

Bath, Aquae Sulis, was as is well-known the popular health resort of Roman Britain. Here we have evidence of the erection of Roman buildings there even before Agricola's time.

[1] If art may be considered an index of national vigour, it is illuminating to compare such purely Celtic work as the splendid pre-Roman enamels or the Castor pottery of the late Roman period, with the attempts of British artists to produce 'classical' work. One is left with the indelible impression that the British genius has been diverted, to its own great detriment, into a stagnant Mediterranean canal. In some few works, such as the Gorgon at Bath, the spirit of a once vigorous barbarism half breaks through the stale Hellenistic convention; and that is all. Cf. C. Jullian's great *Histoire de la Gaule*, v, pp. 553ff, for the equally deplorable effect of Roman rule there. (1967: But Professor J. M. C. Toynbee in her works on Roman Art in Britain takes a more favourable view.)

City Centre at Verulamium

A fragment of Agricola's own name has now been found at St. Albans. In 1955 excavators found four fragments of what must have been a huge inscription about four metres long, running across the face of a public building in the town centre. The first two include part of the top edge of the slab, and the last a piece of the bottom.

40)   (*a*) ·VESPA   (*b*) F·VE
                       DESI

  (*c*) SIAN   MI
       OMN
       GRI   (*d*) O PR
       VE   NATA

JRS, 1956

Not much, it might be thought, from which to restore a continuous text; but experience of the imperial style from numerous continental inscriptions enables experts to do so with fair confidence. VESPA and F·VE in the top line show that the emperor is Titus Vespasianus, son of Vespasianus, who reigned after the death of his father from 79 to 81. SIAN and MI in line 3, which have been chiselled out, leaving traces, are part of the name of Titus' younger brother, Domitian, defaced as usual; and the letters GRI belong to that of Agricola, governor throughout Titus' short reign, and VE, below, probably to that of Verulamium. O PR, finally, will be the end of 'Legato Aug. pro pr(aetore)', and -NATA, requiring something in the feminine, might represent 'basilica ornata', 'on the monumental building of the pillared court-house'. The whole has been reconstructed thus:

IMP · TITO · CAESARI · DIVI · **VESPA**SIANI · **F** · VESPASIANO · A V G
PM· TR· P·VIIII·IMP· XV·COS· VII·**DESIG**·VIII·CENSORI· PATRI· PATRIAE
ET·CAESARI·DIVI·VESPA**SIANI**·F·DO**MI**TIANO·COS·VI·DESIG·VII·PRINCIPI
IUVENTVTIS · ET · **OMN**IVM · COLLEGIORVM · SACERDOTI
CN · IVLIO · **AGRI**COLA · LEGATO · AVG · PRO · **PR**
MVNICIPIVM · **VE**RVLAMIVM · BASILICA · OR**NATA**

S. Frere, *Britannia*, p. 202 (fig. 9)

'*To the Emperor Titus Caesar Vespasianus, son of the deified Vespasian, Augustus, Pontifex Maximus, in the ninth year of his tribunician power, fifteen times saluted Imperator, Consul for the seventh and consul-*

*designate for the eighth time, Censor, Father of his Country; and to the
Caesar, son of the deified Vespasian, Domitian, Consul for the sixth and
designate for the seventh time, Chief of the Youth and member of all the
priestly orders; under Gnaeus Julius Agricola, His Majesty's Lieutenant-
Governor, the Corporation of Verulamium, on completion of the
Basilica (set up this inscription).'*

The Walls of York

41)

IM]P   **CAESA**[R   DIVI
N]**ERVAE FIL** N[ERVA TRA
IA]**NVS AVG GER** [DACICVS
PO]**NTIFEX MAXIMV**[S TRIB
PO]**TESTATIS XII IMP VII** [PP
P]**ER LEG VIIII HI**[SPANAM.

665

'*Imperator Caesar, son of the deified Nerva Traianus, Augustus,
Germanicus, Dacicus, Pontifex Maximus, in the twelfth year of his reign,
seven times hailed Imperator, Father of his Country (built this gate) by
the agency of the Ninth Legion, Hispana.*'

The date is 108, or after Dec. 9, 107.

Its energies set free by the cessation of the wars of conquest, the
Ninth proceeds to adorn and fortify its base with permanent
stone walls and gates; this fine slab was probably erected over one
of the latter. The broken edges can be restored with confidence.

Trajan, the popular soldier adopted by the aged Emperor
Nerva and designated as his successor, naturally takes his
'father's' name in addition to his own. He bears the title Germanicus for his early campaigns on the Rhine, Dacicus for the
two wars culminating in the conquest of the Dacian kingdom by
106.

Civil Life at Wroxeter

42)

IMP · CA[E]·S DIVI · TRAIANI · PARTHI
CI · FIL · DI[VI · N]ERVAE · NEPOTI · TRA
IANO · H[A]DRIANO · AVG · PONTI[FI
CI·MAXIMO·TRIB·POT·XIII[I·COS III·PP
CIVITAS CORNOV[IORVM·

288

*'To the Emperor, Caesar, son of the deified Traianus Parthicus, grandson
of the deified Nerva, Traianus Hadrianus Augustus, Pontifex Maximus,
in the fourteenth year of his reign, thrice Consul, Father of his Country, the
Canton of the Cornovii (erect this).'*

Very finely cut, and the largest complete Roman inscription
found in Britain. The stone measures twelve feet by four, and
the letters are eight inches high.

The senate voted Trajan the further *agnomen* of Parthicus after
his capture of the Parthian capitals at the very end of his reign.
Since the departure of the legions, Viroconium has evidently
developed on normal lines as a market town and the capital of
the Cornovii, the tribe extending over Shropshire and Cheshire.
The date is A.D. 131.

A Wroxeter Family

A curious triple tombstone, with three panels, the left and central
of which bear epitaphs:

43)   (*a*) Left   (*b*) Centre

D	·	M	D · M
P L A C I D A			D E V C C V
AN · LV			S · AN · XV
CVR · AG			CVR · AG
CONI · A			F R A T R E
XXX			

295

(*a*) *'Here lies Placida, aged 55. (This stone was set up) by her husband, in
the thirtieth year (of their marriage).'*

CVR. AG., etc. = *curam agente coniuge, anno tricesimo.*
(*b*) *'Here lies Deuccus, aged 15. Set up by his brother.'*

The third panel remains blank. No doubt it was intended to
receive the epitaph of a third member of the family, but was
never used.

The fact that this British woman and boy have each only one
name, whether Latin like Placida or Celtic like Deuccus, shows
that they are not Roman citizens; but they are clearly, to judge by
the typical Latin phrases on this family tombstone, Romanising
as fast as they can.

THE ROMAN ROADS
NEAR LEICESTER

44)   IMP·CAES
        DIV·TRAIAN·PARTH·F·DIV[I·NERV]·NEP
        TRAIAN · HADRIAN · AVG ·P· P· T[RI]B
                POT·IV·COS·III·A·RATIS
                          H

2244

THE HOLYHEAD ROAD

45)   IMP · CAES · TRAI
                    ANVS·HADRIANVS
                    AVG·P·M·TR·P·V
                    · P · P · COS · III
                    A · K A N O V I O
                    ·M·P·VIII

2265

Two of the earliest British examples of the large though
roughly inscribed Roman milestones.

'*Imperator Caesar, son of the deified Traianus Parthicus, grandson of the
deified Nerva, Traianus Hadrianus Augustus, Father of his Country, in
the fourth year of his reign, thrice Consul. Two miles to Leicester.*'

Dated A.D. 121. Leicester was Ratae of the Coritani, a small
market town at a cross-roads. The H = II.

'*Imperator Caesar Traianus Hadrianus Augustus, Pontifex Maximus,
in the fifth year of his reign, Father of his Country, Thrice Consul.
Conway, eight miles.*'

M.P. = *milia passum*, 'thousands of [double] paces' (of five feet).
The name Conway is, of course, simply 'Canovium' slightly
altered; the Roman station was, however, actually a few miles
inland, at Caerhyn.

§2   BRITONS WRITE IN LATIN

There is no more striking evidence of the Romanisation of the
southern Britons than the fact that Latin and not Welsh seems to
have been the common speech of all classes in the towns. In
Gaul, curiously enough, where the traces of Latin civilisation are
much more imposing, we do find an occasional Celtic inscription;

in Britain until the Empire was crumbling, not one. Latin is invariably used, even in the most casual scribble, by people in quite humble walks of life. The following fragments of letters and legal documents from London, in the Guildhall Museum, are all found on fragments of the wood of writing-tablets, originally covered with wax and hinged together in pairs, with raised edges on the sides meant to fold together. They were convenient for temporary memoranda or short notes, as they could be tied with tape and sealed for privacy, and also used time after time; the letters could be erased with the flat butt end of the pointed metal pencil or *stilus*, and also new coats of wax could be supplied indefinitely. When the wax was wearing thin the stilus sometimes scored the wood; hence we can read these scraps of writing, much as we might decipher the letters on a blotting-pad.

46)
> *quam pecuniam petisionis item*
> *scriptis solvere mihi debebit cres-*
> *cens isve ad quem ea res per-*
> *tinebit Id · · · ·-retris(?) primis*

petisionis: a mistake or abbreviation for *petionibus*? If so:

'—— this money when the applications have been redrafted will be owed to me by Crescens or the party concerned; payment due (on the Ides ——?) —— first.'

47)
> *· · · · · rem vendidisse · · · · · · · ·*
> *ex taberna sua · · · · · · · · · · · · ·*
> *· · · · · · · · · · · · · navem faci·*
> *endam et permissionem dedisse*
> *· · · · · · · · · · · · · clavi faciendi*

'—— to have sold goods —— from his own shop —— a ship to be built, and to have given permission —— of making a rudder.'

48)
> [*per Iov-*]
> *em optimum maximum et per ge-*
> *nium Imp. Domitiani Cesaris Aug. Ge-*
> *rmanici et per deos patrios su[os?]*

Formula of an oath: '—— by Jupiter the Best and Greatest, and by the Spirit of the Emperor Domitianus Cesar Augustus Germanicus and by their (or his) own ancestral gods ——'

Cesar: *e* for *ae* becomes quite common as a vulgarism under the Empire.

For the above, see London Museum Catalogue No. 3, *London in Roman Times*; *RIB* II, forthcoming. But the longest such fragment, discovered in 1927 in the Walbrook, was deciphered by Richmond only much later (published in *Antiquaries' Journal* XXXIII, 1953; *JRS* XLIV, 1954): Outside, in large letters:

49)   LONDINIO
               LVITA AD S [VOS?]

Inside:

> *Rufus Callisuni salutem Epillico et omni*
> *bus contubernalibus certiores vos esse*
> *credo me recte valere si vos indi*
> *cem fecistis rogo mittite omnia*
> *diligenter cura agas ut illam puel*
> *lam ad nummum redigas* . . . . .

There was probably more, but it is uncertain. The Latin is illiterate and there is no sign of punctuation; but the following translation may be hazarded. The outside is part of an address:

'*(Dated) from London. Luita to (his partners?)* . . .'

'*Rufus (son?) of Callisunus (sends) greeting to Epillicus and all the partners. I think you know that I am quite well. If you have gone to law (?), please send me all details carefully. See to it that you turn that girl into cash.*'

In line 2, the writer seems to confuse the phrases '*certiores vos facio*', 'I inform you' and '*scire vos credo*', 'I think you know'. In 3, 4, *indicem fecistis* defies translation, but he may have meant '*indicium*', 'evidence against', so 'a charge'. The reference to a (slave-)girl sounds as if the *contubernales* ('living-companions', 'partners'?) have been quarrelling over her.

Two Curses

Two small texts draw our attention to the seamy side of life.

If in the classical world one wished to do someone an injury (as many did), and physical methods were not available, one wrote the enemy's name on a scrap of lead, often stolen from a building, usually with the words 'is fixed' or 'I fix', and nailed the tablet

down, often to a tomb. This was considered to *devote* or 'vow'
the victim to the gods of the underworld. It is obviously connected with the primitive superstition about names, that the
name *is* the man. Thus, on both sides of such a scrap, now in the
London Museum:

50) (*a*) *T·Egnativs*   (*b*) *TEgnativs*
           Tyranvs deficvs (*sic*)   *Tyranvs defictvs*
                 est et   *est et*
           PCicereivs Felix   *P Cicereivs Felix*
           defictvs est

6, a, b

'*Titus Egnatius Tyranus* (*sic*) *is fixed and Publius Cicereius Felix is
fixed.*'

In (*b*) the writer was getting tired before he had done 'defictus
est' for the fourth time.

A more elaborate and furious example is in the British Museum:

51)   *Tretia Maria defico et*
                       illevs vita et metem
                       et memoriam t iocine
                       ra pvlmones intermxixi
                       ta fata cogitata memor
                       iam sci no possitt loqvi
                       sicreta sit neqve · ·

7

Letters are omitted (e.g final *m* in the name, which must be
accusative; *n* in *mentem*, line 2, *e* of *et* and final *n* of *non* in 3 and 6);
added (doubled *t* in *possitt*) (6); transposed (*sci* for *sic*, in 6, and
perhaps in the name Tretia, which is rare, for the common
Tertia?); while when he came to write *intermixta*, his apparent
intention in 4-5, he became decidedly 'mixed up' himself. The
tablet was also transfixed with no less than seven nails. Nevertheless, Collingwood and Wright have thus deciphered the cursive
writing:

'*I fix Tertia* (?) *Maria and her life and mind and memory and liver and
lungs mixed, fate, thoughts, memory; so may she not be able to speak
secrets nor . . .*'

There was a little more, but it defeats even the experts. For 'fate', Mr Wright would understand 'words'; but would this semi-literate person have known this rare original meaning of *fata*?

Some scribbles on pottery by workmen and others will all be published in *RIB* II. A selection follows:

A pair from London:

52)
>   *Austalis*
>   *dibus xiii*
>   *vagatur sib*
>   *cotidim*

Possibly '*Austalis has been wandering about by himself every day for a fortnight.*' *Dibus* probably = *diebus; sib, sibi; cotidim, cotidie.* Probably a workman's comment on the slackness of another (scratched in the wet clay of the tile Austalis has just left?)

53)
>   *·LONDINI*
>   *AD FANUM ISIDIS*

This, of which we have now two specimens, is the address of a public house. '*London; next door to the temple of Isis.*' (Cf. *ad urbem*, 'just outside the city'—*at*, but not *in*.) Scratched on a jug, this time after the clay was dry; that is to say, the words give the address 'not of the potter, but of the wine-merchant who bottled the contents' (Haverfield).

A pair from Leicester:

54)
>   *Primus fecit x*

'*Primus has made ten*'—on the wet clay of a tile; presumably by the maker.

55)
>   V E R E C V N D A
>   L V D I A   L V C
>   I V S   G L A D I A
>   TOR

'*Verecunda the actress: Lucius the gladiator.*'

Scratched with extreme care on a fragment of pottery, these names look like a relic of a romance. Actresses and gladiators on tour in a remote province would normally be slaves. Did these two forgotten entertainers, meeting by chance, write their names together on this and another potsherd to be a keepsake, in the hope that one day they might win their freedom and meet again?

A group from Silchester:

56)
Pertacus perfidus
campester Lucilianus
Campanus conticuere omnes

'Perfidious Pertacus—plain-dweller—Lucilianus—Campanian—they all fell silent.'

A jumble of proper names and other words, giving no connected sense, 'possibly part of a writing-lesson' (Haverfield), ending with a well-known tag from the opening of the second book of the Aeneid.

57)
vi k octo
Manuicc

A date; '*Sixth day before the kalends of October*' (Sept. 26) and a name, Manuicc(us?)

58) ——*puellam* '*Girl*.' The tile is broken off. 'No doubt part of an amatory sentence' (Haverfield).

59) *fur* '*Thief*'; scratched on a bit of 'Samian' ware—the red Gallic pottery with embossed ornamentation, that was the universal 'best china' of every middle-class household; 'presumably as a warning from the servants of one house to those of the next' (Haverfield).

And finally, two written with the finger tip-by workmen at the local brickworks, on the still wet clay:

60) *Fecit tubul Clementinus.* (*tubul = tubulum.*)
   '*Clementinus made this box-tile.*'

61) *Satis.* '*Fed up.*' (or '*stint completed*'?)

A TRAVELLING LECTURER

One result of Romanisation was naturally a demand for schoolmasters and lecturers, to initiate the Briton into the mysteries of Latin and Greek literature, and to teach him the tricks of the rhetoric which the Romans so deplorably regarded as the fine flower of a gentleman's education. We have allusions in Latin writers—both Juvenal and Martial, for instance—to the way in which Britain, following the example of Gaul, Spain and Africa, was imbibing Roman oratory. 'Eloquent Gaul has taught the Britons to plead a case', cries Juvenal[1]; 'by now, Ultima Thule talks of hiring a rhetorician!' And Plutarch, in his essay 'On the Cessation of Oracles,' mentions how he met at Delphi in A.D. 83 a Greek teacher of rhetoric, named Demetrius, who had just come back from lecturing in Britain. Demetrius told him how he had been sent 'on an official mission' to some of the remoter British islands, and had found on one of them a community of 'holy men', unmolested by the warlike peoples around them, who were ready to tell him about their theories on meteorology and mythology (a fascinating anticipation of Christian Irish monasticism). The date would well fit Agricola's Irish Sea explorations of A.D. 82, on which Demetrius may have been taken as a civilian observer.

It is therefore quite possibly this same Demetrius who dedicated at York two little bronze tablets, silver-gilt, which were discovered in 1840 in the laying out of the site of the old railway station:

62)	(a)	(b)
	Θεοις	Ωκεανωι
	τοις του ηγε	και Τηθυι
	μονικου πραι	Δημητρι(ος)
	τωριου Σκριβ	
	(Δ)η(μ)ητριος	
	662	663

(*a*) '*To the Gods of the Governor's Praetorium, Scribonius Demetrius (dedicates this).*'

ἡγέμων = Governor—as in N.T. etc. Σκριβ, formerly understood as *scriba*, secretary, is perhaps more probably Demetrius' Roman-citizen family name Scribonius.

(*b*) '*To Ocean and Tethys, Demetrius (dedicates this).*'

Tethys is the old Greek mother-goddess of the teeming life of the sea, sometimes called wife of Oceanus.

(*a*) is therefore a patriotic dedication; (*b*) probably pays a vow made for a safe return from the dedicator's voyage to the western islands. (*a*) measures three by two inches; (*b*) is still smaller.

---

[1] *Satires*, xv, ll. 111-12.

A Roman Crossword

Scratched on the plaster of a Roman house-wall at Cirencester is an ingenious example of a word square:

63)

                    R O T A S
                    O P E R A
                    T E N E T
                    A R E P O
                    S A T O R

It was very popular and is found at many other places in the Empire. By taking AREPO as a proper name in the nominative (it is not otherwise known), the words can be read as a sentence: *'Arepo the Sower holds the wheels at work.'* Now the letters can be rearranged, as here, to form the words PATER NOSTER,

                         P
                         A
              A   T   O
                         E
                         R
        P A T E R N O S T E R
                         O
                         S
              A   T   O
                         E
                         R

crossing at the N, with an additional A and O—Alpha and Omega, —twice over; though this arrangement does not seem actually to be found. It has therefore been suggested that the word-square was a Christian secret symbol. This is not proven, and if it was so it was invented very early, since it appears at Herculaneum, overwhelmed in the eruption of 79. But it certainly was *taken up* by Christians, and survived as a charm even into the middle ages.

A Country Feud

One more example of the use of Latin—this time very much later—even in the country. The inscription is on a small tablet of pewter, about three inches by two and a half, and comes from

Lydney Park, Gloucestershire. It was evidently dedicated at the shrine of a local deity, Nodens, which flourished in the late fourth century. Someone, having lost a ring, and strongly suspecting an enemy, one of the neighbours, but not quite venturing to make an accusation, adopts this method of telling the god all about it, offering him a handsome reward for its recovery and adding a most vindictive prayer.

64)

DEVO	
NODENTI	SILVIANVS
ANILVM	PERDEDIT
DEMEDIAM	PARTEM
DONAVIT	NODENTI
INTER QVIBVS NOMEN	
SENICIANI	NOLLIS
PETMITTAS	SANITA
TEM DONEC PERFERAT	
VSQUE TEMPLVM [NO]	
DENTIS.	

306

'To the god Nodens. Silvianus has lost a ring. He has dedicated half of it to Nodens. Among those who bear the name of Senicianus, please grant no health until he brings it to the temple of Nodens.'

The spelling and grammar are original. The most curious error, *petmittas for permittas*, is perhaps due to the fact that T and R are not very unlike in Roman cursive writing, though the inscription is in block capitals.

§3 TRADE, LOCAL GOVERNMENT, PROFESSIONS

65)

DEAE·TVTELE BOVDIG
M·AVR·LVNARIS III III
VIR·AVG·COL·EBOR·ET
LIND · PROV · BRIT · INF
ARAM · QVAM · VOVER
AB EBORACI AVECT
V·S·L·M
PERPETVO ET CORNE

Inscription on an altar found at Bordeaux.

'To the protecting goddess Boudig, Marcus Aurelius Lunaris, Sevir Augustalis of the Colonies of York and Lincoln in the Province of Lower Britain, (dedicates) the altar which he had vowed when he sailed from York. He pays his vow willingly and duly. Consulship of Perpetuus and Cornelianus.' (A.D. 237).

Eboraci is a slip, for *Eboraco*.

'The goddess Boudig' clearly gives us the derivation of the human name Boudicca.

The name Aurelius becomes so common after the reigns of the two great Aurelii Antonini that it is regularly abbreviated; compare the name Flavius in No. 74. The reason is that anyone receiving Roman citizenship took the *nomen* of his patron as his own *nomen* and kept his individual name as a *cognomen*; cf. Ti. Claudius Cogidubnus in No. 2. A freedman took the name of his old master, and people enfranchised by the emperor took his.

A *sevir Augustalis* was a member of the chapter of six men appointed in every corporate town to superintend the official cult of the emperor. Augustus, laid open the position to freedmen, whose servile origin excluded them from so many positions of social prestige; many of them were 'self-made' men of substance, for the same qualities that had won them their freedom stood in good stead in business, and it was a clever stroke thus to attach them by bonds of sentiment to the throne. *Augustales* had need to be men of substance, for the upkeep of the cult had to be paid for; so the fact that Lunaris is a *sevir* makes it likely that he is a rich freedman.

Severus, early in the third century, divided several provinces including Britain, into two, Upper and Lower, in order to reduce the powers of the governors. No one tells us what the boundary was, but this inscription shows that York and Lincoln were in Lower Britain; as we know from other inscriptions that Aesica (Great Chesters) on Hadrian's Wall was in the Lower, and Chester and Caerleon in the Upper province, it appears that the boundary ran from Lincolnshire to Lancashire, south-east to north-west.

A tombstone from Bordeaux also testifies to this Atlantic coasting trade:

R.B.—E

66)   D   M
                          L·SOLIMARIO
                          SECVNDINO
                          CIVITREVERO
                          NEG · BRITAN
CIL XIII, 634

Since the deceased is not a Briton but a Trever from the Rhineland, *Neg.Britan.* should be expanded as *negotiatori Britanniciano*, 'a merchant in the British trade', for which there is authority in an inscription from the Rhineland. *Solimario* represents a German type of name ending in *-mar*.

LOCAL GOVERNMENT
THE CANTON OF THE SILURES

67)   [T I · C L A VDIO]
                          P A V L I N O
                          L E G · L E G · II
                          A V G · P R O C O N SVL
                          P R O V I N C · N A R
                          R B O N E N S I S
                          LEG·AVG·PR·PR·PROVIN
                          L V G V D V N E N
                          EX   ·   D E C R E T O
                          O R D I N I S   ·   R E S
                          P V B L   ·   C I V I T
                          S I L V R V M
311

From Caerwent (Venta Silurum); an inscription in honour of a distinguished senator who in his earlier days had commanded the Second Legion at Isca, twelve miles away; the name is lost, but the career corresponds with that of one Claudius Paulinus, known from an inscription in France, who lived in the first half of the third century. The inscription is our most direct evidence from Britain of the great Roman system of 'home rule' by local councils. True, democracy was not tolerated, and political institutions were all adapted to the Roman model, just as we find here that the council has become a (*senatorius*) *ordo*, a Senatorial Order. The inscription is probably an act of gratitude to an officer who had done some kindness to the natives among whom he had once lived, such as sponsoring some petition which the *res publica* of the Silures wished to present to the emperor.

The lines are kept roughly the same length by a liberal and ingenious use of ligatured letters—a habit which becomes prevalent and often irritating in the third century. The R of NARBONENSIS is repeated by a mistake. Translation:

'To Tiberius Claudius Paulinus, Commander of Legion II Augusta, Proconsul of the Province of (Gallia) Narbonensis, Imperial Pro-Praetorian Legate of the Province of (Gallia) Lugudunensis, by decree of their Senate the Commonwealth of the State of the Silures (erect this).'

Notice the distinction of title of the senatorial province of Narbonese Gaul (Provence); *Legatus Augusti Pro Praetore* of the Imperial province of central Gaul or Lugdunensis (to use the commoner spelling).

THE COLONY OF YORK

68)   D   M
        FLAVI·BELLATORIS·DEC·COL·EBORACENS
        VIXIT ANNIS · XXVIII · MENSIB · · · · ·
             (broken away at bottom)

674

'To the memory of Flavius Bellator, City Councillor of the Colony of Eboracum. He lived for 28 years · · · months [and · · · days · · ·]'

Inscription on a stone coffin at York, containing a skeleton, of small stature, still wearing his official gold ring, set with a ruby.

The *decuriones*, or members of the city council, were elected from among the richer citizens. Their chief duty towards the central government was to produce the sum at which the local taxes were assessed. They were also responsible for collecting the sum due, from the inhabitants at large; but if they failed to collect so much, the loss was theirs. Under the later empire the risk of having to bear the loss oneself became so grave that the honourable position of Decurion ceased to be popular.

INDUSTRY

Among the lead and silver mines of Britain none were more

important than those of Derbyshire, from which we have numerous stamped pigs of lead of the second or third centuries. Here are the inscriptions on three:

69) (*a*) IMP·CAES·HADRIANI·AVG·MET·LVT·—From Wirksworth, Derbyshire. '*Property of Imperator Caesar Hadrianus Augustus; from the mines of Lutudarum.*'
    Lutudarum was probably somewhere near Matlock.

   (*b*) C·IVL·PROTI·BRIT·LVT·EX·ARG.—From Hexgrave Park, near Mansfield. '*Property of Gaius Julius Protus; British lead from Lutudarum, from the silver mines*', or perhaps '*de-silverised lead*'.

   (*c*) P·RVBRI·ABASCANT·METALLI·LVTVDARES·—From Tansley Moor, near Matlock. '*Property of Publius Rubrius Abascantus, from the mines of Lutudarum.*'

   METALLI LVTVDARES = *metallis Lutudarensibus*, slightly abbreviated.
BM, pp. 30f

THE MEDICAL PROFESSION: AN OCULIST

We shall meet with some army doctors in our section on the life of the military area; in the civil area of Britain the chief relics of the medical profession that we have are a number of stone stamps used by commercial chemists for impressing their names probably on solid cakes of ointment—especially, it seems, ointment for the eyes. Here, as a sample, are the inscriptions cut on the four sides of a little flat slab of stone, found at Sandy, Bedfordshire:

70)
(*a*) C.VAL.AMANDI.DIOXVM AD RHEVMATICA
(*b*) C.VAL.AMANDI.STACTVM AD CALIGINEM
(*c*) C·VAL·VALENTINI DIAGLAVCIVM POST IMPETVM LIPPITVDINIS
(*d*) MIXTVM AD CLARITUDINEM
B.M, p. 33

(*a*) '*Gaius Valerius Amandus' Vinegar-lotion for running eyes.*'
(*b*) '*Gaius Valerius Amandus' Drops for dim sight.*'
(*c*) '*Gaius Valerius Valentinus' Poppy-ointment after an attack of inflammation of the eyes.*'
(*d*) '*A mixture for clearing the sight.*'

At least one British oculist, a certain Stolus, was eminent

enough for his collyrium to be mentioned by Galen (Claudius Galēnus), the last great name in the history of ancient European medicine.

§4 BRITAIN AND THE ARMY

British cavalry and infantry regiments (cf. No. 36) gained a high reputation in the Roman army. Lists of the troops in the Danubian provinces record the names and serial numbers of many, and in Trajan's Dacian Wars several won the distinction of being made Roman Citizens before their discharge, or other titles of honour. A unique 'diploma' from Dacia is a British soldier's personal copy (no doubt he paid for it) of a decree of Trajan, dated from an unknown place, perhaps a Dacian battlefield:

71) IMP·CAES·DIV·NERV·F·NERVA·TRAI·AVG·GER·DAC·
PONT·MAX· TR·P·XIIII·IMP·VI· COS·V· P·P·
PEDITIBVS ET EQVITIBVS QVI MILITANT IN COH·I
BRITTONVM M·VLPIA TORQVATA P·F· C·R· QVAE
EST IN DACIA SVB D·TERENTIO SCAVRIANO, QVORVM
NN· SVBSCRIPTA SVNT, PIE ET FIDELITER EXPEDITIONE
DACICA FVNCTIS, ANTE EMERITA STIPENDIA CIV·R·DEDIT·

A.D.III IDVS AVG.
DARNITHITHI
L. MINICIO NATALE
Q. SILVANO GRANIANO   COS

PEDITI
M.VLPIO ADCOBROVATI F. NOVANTICO[NI]RATIS

'The Emperor Caesar, son of the deified Nerva, Nerva Traianus Augustus, Conqueror of the Germans and the Dacians, Pontifex Maximus, in the fourteenth (sic) year of his Tribunician Power, six times saluted Imperator, five times Consul, Father of his Country.

To the infantry and cavalry soldiers serving in the 1st Cohort of Britons, 1000 strong, Trajan's Own, Decorated with the torquis, Loyal and True, Roman Citizens, which is in Dacia under Decimus Terentius Scaurianus, whose names are hereto appended,

Has granted Roman citizenship for loyal and true service in the Dacian campaign, before the completion of their service.

This third day before the Ides of August (Aug. 11)
    at Darnithithis
in the consulship of
    L. Minicius Natalis and (A.D. 106)
Q. Silvanus Granianus

    To Private
Marcus Ulpius Novantico, son of Adcobrovatus, from Leicester.'

The copying of a rare type of document did not go through without some errors, of which 'TR.P.XIIII' is one. It would appear that Novantico was discharged and wanted his copy of his title to citizenship in Trajan's fourteenth year, our 110; and the scribe inadvertently wrote down the number of that year instead of the final year of the Second Dacian War as shown by the names of the consuls. And in giving Novantico's name, he wrote 'Novantico', which looked like a dative, and only then noticed that *-co*, and not *-cus*, was the nominative. Having already written 'Rati(s)', he then had to squeeze in the letters '-ni' above the line. Which of us has not made similar mistakes in his time?

To this may be appended a couple of the rather rare inscriptions set up by Britons (or soldiers in originally British regiments) themselves:

A DEDICATION

72)
    N Y M P H I S   N
    B R I T T O N ·
    T R I P V T I E N ·
    S V B   C V R A
    M   ·   VLPI   MALC
    HI 〉 LEG XXII PR.P.F.

D 2624

'To the Nymphs (this altar is dedicated by) the Triputiensian British Irregulars, under the command of Marcus Ulpius Malchus, centurion in the Twenty-Second Legion, Primigenia, Pia, Fidelis.'

Triputium was probably the place on the upper Danube where the unit was stationed.

N. stands for *numerus*, literally 'number'. Originally the irregular light infantry, which the army needed in frontier wars in wild country, had been supplied by the auxiliary cohorts. As time went on these became more and more 'regular' until their discipline and drill almost rivalled that of the legions. But something was lost of their old qualities for guerilla warfare, and the government then raised new irregular regiments from the wilder parts of the Empire, called *Numeri*. They begin to appear in inscriptions during the second century.

The centurion seconded from his legion to command them bears a Phoenician or Jewish name—compare, for instance, *St. John*, xviii, 10. The Roman part of his name shows that his family had received Roman citizenship from Trajan. The inscription will be not earlier than a third century; Orientals rarely appear as centurions in western legions earlier than that.

The meaning of the legion's title, Primigenia, is disputed; but probably it derives from the legion's formation by dividing an old legion having the same number (XXII Deiotariana) into two, thus providing two *cadres* which could be filled up with recruits. Of the two legions thus formed, one, it is assumed, received the old legion's title, the other the old legion's eagle and the title Primigenia—'First-Born'.

The titles 'Loyal and True' were conferred by Domitian on a large number of units of the Rhine army which remained loyal at the time of the abortive revolt of Saturninus in Upper Germany in 89.

AN EPITAPH

73)

```
        D              M
    C A T A V I G N I
    I V O M A G I  ·  F
    M I L I T I      COH
    III          BRITAN
    NORVM   )   GESATI
    VIX  ·  ANN  ·  XXV
    STI  ·  VI  ·  EXERCI
    TVS          RAETICI
    P A T E R N V S
    H        F        C
    C O M M I L I T O N I
    C A R I S S I M O
```

D 2560

From Raetia, the province that stretched from the Alps to the upper Danube:

'*To the Gods of the Underworld. To Catavignes, son of Ivomagus, soldier in the Third British Cohort, Gesatus' Company, who lived for twenty-five years and served for six, in the Army of Raetia. Paternus his heir set this up, to his fellow-soldier and good friend.*'

A BRITISH CENTURION?

Not many Britons, natives as they were of a remote and backward province, rose to the rank of centurion, at any rate under the early Empire. One, however, who died old in the third century at Lambaesis in Africa, was probably British:

74)
```
              D               M
T' FL · VIRILIS ⟩ LEG II AVG
⟩ LEG XX V V ⟩ LEG VI VIC
⟩ LEG XX V V ⟩ LEG III AVG
⟩ LEG III PARTH · SEVER
VIIII   HAST   ·   POSTER
V I X I T   A N N I S   L X X
S T I P  X X X X V  L O L L I A
B O D I C C A      C O N I V X
E T  F L A V I  V I C T O R  E T
V I C T O R I N V S     F I L I
H E R E D E S    E X    H S
M C C   N   F A C I E N D V M
         C V R A V E R ·
```

JRS II (1912)

'(*Dis Manibus.*) *Tiberius Flavius Virilis, Centurion in Legion II Augusta, Centurion in Legion XX Valeria Victrix, Centurion in Legion VI Victrix, Centurion in Legion XX Valeria Victrix, Centurion in Legion III Augusta, Centurion in Legion III Parthica, Emperor Severus' Own, commanding the Second Century of Hastati of Cohort VIIII, lived for 70 years and served for 45. Lollia Bodicca his wife, and Flavius Victor and Flavius Victorinus his sons, his heirs, had this monument set up at a cost of 1200 sesterces.*'

Virilis serves as centurion with the legions at Caerleon, at Chester, at York (where the Sixth replaced the Ninth early in the second century, see Nos. 96-97, below) again at Chester, then is sent out of the province to the Third, Augusta, stationed at Lambaesis, then to the Third, Parthica, one of the three new legions raised by Severus for his Parthian Wars, and finally returns to spend his last days at Lambaesis again.

The position of centurion of the rear-rank *hastati* of the Ninth Cohort—the junior century of the last cohort but one—is presumably mentioned as the highest post that Virilis filled. It does not sound a very high one, for a centurion's sixth post; but it seems likely that there were centurions of two kinds, which might be called commissioned and non-commissioned. The former might be re-enlisted guardsmen, like Vettius Valens in No. 16, or Roman *equites*, men of some standing in civil life (No. 98). These, it is suggested, were promoted rapidly and might reach full commissioned rank, or hold imperial procuratorships, or the immensely important post of *primus pilus*. (This is the *locuples aquila*, the lucrative post that involves guardianship of the Eagle, of Juvenal xiv, 197.) On the other hand, ranker-centurions are promoted only slowly; thus Virilis in his sixth centurionate is only seven steps from the bottom of the ladder.

The second name of Virilis' wife is the same as that of the famous queen of the Iceni. Lollia, her Latin family-name, suggests that her people received the citizenship from Lollius Urbicus, the soldier-governor of Britain in 141-3 (No. 116).

N, in the last line but one = *nummis*, sesterces, and after the word HS, *sestertiis*, in the previous line, is not really needed.

THE GARRISON TOWNS

As the frontier became stable, the legions, remaining in one place for decade after decade, came to feel themselves more and more a local garrison, less and less a field army. It was to prove a dangerous tendency; but that was far in the future; for the present the most noticeable point is the development of civil life at the garrison towns—not only at the Colonies of Lincoln and Gloucester, where the troops had been, but at that of York, where a legion remained, and at Caerleon and Chester which were not colonies. Inscriptions from all three show us discharged soldiers settling down close to the barracks in which they had served, rather than return to a home which they had not seen for twenty years. Even soldiers who were still serving often married and had children, though the marriages of serving soldiers were not officially recognised until the time of Severus. Even after that time, women were not permitted within the sacred precincts of the 'camp', and had to live outside. Thus the legionary fortress became the nucleus of a town, with a population of discharged soldiers and their families, soldiers' wives, children and slaves, and numerous traders and other civilians serving the forces.

A Very Old Soldier

75)

[D   M]
IVL . VALENS · VET
LEG · II · AVG · VIXIT
ANNIS · C · I V L
SECVNDINA · CONIVNX
ET·IVL·MARTINVS·FILIVS
F   C

363

A tombstone from Caerleon, broken at the top.

'*Julius Valens, Veteran of Legion II Augusta, lived 100 years. Julia Secundina his wife and Julius Martinus his son had this made.*'

Vixit annis becomes commoner than classical *annos* under the empire.

A Freedman

76)

D   M
ET ACONTIO
LIBERTO   BENE
MERENTI · C · ASV
RIVS FORTI · PATR
ONVS EIVS POSVIT

(Chester)

559

'*To the Gods of the Underworld, and to Acontius his freedman, well deserving; Gaius Asurius Fortis his master set this up.*'

D M ET ACONTIO is a curious expression, and unparalleled. The gap on the stone between ET and ACONTIVS is very small, and

MITHRAS IN LONDON

By kind permission of the Trustees of the London Museum

Plate 2

possibly we ought to read 'Etacontius'; but if so, it is a strange name and not otherwise known.

A Soldier's Child

77)
D · M· SIMPLICIAE · FLORENTINE
ANIME · INNOCENTISSIME
QVE · VIXIT · MENSES · DECEM
FELICIVS·SIMPLEX·PATER·FECIT
LEG·VI·V

690 (York)

'*To the Gods Below. To Simplicia Florentina, a most innocent soul, who lived ten months; Felicius Simplex her father set this up, a soldier in Legion VI Victrix.*'

For the Sixth Legion at York, see below, No. 96n.

Mithras in London

At Londinium too, by far the greatest town in the province and probably replacing Colchester as the administrative capital, there was a small garrison, as well as ex-soldiers and traders. Some of these founded in London a Mithraeum, a chapel of that Persian deity of Light, Truth and Justice, the opponent of the Evil One, the mediator between man and God, the one true Light, who became especially the Roman soldier's god. Hence comes the best-known Mithraic monument found in Britain; a relief, in Italian marble, of the kind that formed the reredos of every Mithraic chapel, of Mithras in his Persian garb and Phrygian cap slaying the mystic bull. On each side and below is a short inscription by the donor:

78)

VLPI	E M E R I
VS	TVS LEG
SILVA	II AVG
NVS	V O T V M
	S O L V I T
FAC	ARAV
TVS	SIONE

3   [See Plate 2]

'*Ulpius Silvanus, Discharged Soldier of Legion II Augusta, pays his vow. Made at Arausio.*'

Arausio is Orange in Provence. (That it means that the sculpture was done at Orange is unlikely.) As probable as any explanation is Collingwood's view, that Silvanus means that he was initiated there into one of the seven grades of the Mithraic 'freemasonry'.

Mithraism, attractive and ethically sound and vigorous as it was, had no place in its system for women. No one, consequently, ever first heard of Mithras from his mother in infancy. This was one of its disadvantages in later conflict with Christianity. There developed however a curious alliance between the religion of Mithras and that of Isis, whose mysteries satisfied for women, as those of Mithras did for men, the craving 'To be a part of one great strength, That moves and cannot die'. It is therefore of interest that we have evidence in Londinium of a temple of Isis too (No. 53).

The Mithraeum was itself discovered in 1953, in Walbrook (the street named after the brook that flowed through the middle of the city), during excavations for the foundations of new buildings on a bombed site. The reredos above had probably been removed from it and buried, to save it from desecration by Christians in the fourth century. But within it was found, rather curiously (also moved in the last days of paganism?), a classical marble group of Bacchus (Dionysus) and his retinue: old Silenus on his donkey, a young satyr, a maenad with a panther. On its foot a later hand had cut, with late Latin phonetic spelling (B, pronounced like our v, for classical v, the u or w sound) the brief prayer:

79)   HOMINIBVS BAGIS BITAM

I

'(*Grant*) *life to men astray.*'

§5   A HEALTH RESORT: THE INSCRIPTIONS OF ROMAN BATH

The inscriptions of most of the towns of Roman Britain—London, York, Chester, for instance—must needs be quoted in this collection in chronological order or under the subjects to which they refer; but there is one town whose inscriptions may fitly be grouped together. Those of the popular little watering-place of Aquae Sulis, taken together, sum up the little town's quiet history rather well.

First we have a large and fine sculptured slab, showing a Roman horseman riding down a barbarian; the tombstone of a cavalry-man, of the same type as those from Gloucester and Cirencester already quoted (Nos. 8, 9). Below come the words:

80)
```
          L  ·  VITELLIVS  ·  MA
          NTAI  ·  F  ·  TANCINVS
          CIVES · HISP · CAVRIESIS
          EQ·ALAE·VETTONVM·C·R
          ANNXXXXVI · STIP · XXVI
          H      ·      S      ·      E
```

159

Lucius Vitellius Tancinus, son of Mantaus, a citizen of Caurium in Spain, Trooper in the Vettonian Regiment of Roman Citizens, who lived for 46 years and served for 26, lies here.

The Vettones were a people of Portugal. Roman citizenship has been conferred on this entire *ala* in reward for its services.

This stone with the early formula H.S.E., *hic situs est*, no doubt dates from early Roman campaigns in the west country.

Next comes the fragment already quoted (No. 39), bearing the words:

· · · · · VES · VII · CO · · · · ·

'· · · · · *Vespasian for the seventh time Consul* · · · ·'

Roman Bath is coming into existence. The date is A.D. 76, and the stone belongs to the gable of a temple or other building, whose erection the inscription recorded.

The popularity of 'the Waters' in the following centuries is well attested by the remains; while the find of a pair of dice, one of which was cogged, serves to assure us that the shadier aspects of life at a fashionable resort were not absent. Romanised Britons, officials, soldiers, all sought rest and recreation at the spa; though the stones naturally record chiefly those who died there.

The tutelary deity of the place was the goddess Sul, whom the Romans identified with Minerva. First among the tombstones we may well place that of her priest—no doubt an important local figure and probably, according to Graeco-Roman practice, manager of the Spa and its convalescent-homes. Chronologically, the stone is shown by the very numerous ligatured letters to be not earlier than the third century.

81)
```
                        D·M
       C        ·        CALPVRNIVS
       [R]ECEPTVS         SACER
       DOS        DEAE        SV
       LIS · VIX · AN · LXXV
       CALPVRNIA      ·      TRIFO
       SA · [LIB · ?] ET · CONIVNX
                        F·C
```
155
'To the Gods of the Underworld. Gaius Calpurnius Receptus, Priest of the Goddess Sul, lived for seventy-five years. Calpurnia Trifosa, his freedwoman and wife, set up this stone.'

The damaged word is probably LIB., *liberta*.

On the two inscriptions which follow, the old antiquary Leland tells us: 'There be divers notable antiquitees engravid in stone that yet be sene yn the walles of Bathe betwixt the southe gate and the west gate, and agayn between the west gate and the north gate.' We are indebted to him for copies of them, for the stones, whether by vandalism or neglect, have since perished.

WHAT ARE MY CHANCES?

A new discovery shows the presence of another ecclesiastical dignitary:

82)
```
              DEAE · SVLI
            L·MARCIVS·MEMOR
               HARVSP
           D        ·        D
```

B. Cunliffe, in *Antiquity*, XL; *JRS* LVII

'To the Goddess Sulis, Lucius Marcius Memor, *haruspex*, dedicated this (*statue*).'

A *haruspex* ('inspector of entrails') was a diviner who, in accordance with ancient Etruscan pseudo-science, interpreted the omens furnished by those of sacrificed beasts. A spa no doubt furnished a suitable public among which such an activity could flourish. It is the first evidence for the existence of professional *haruspices* in Britain.

A GLOUCESTER COUNCILLOR

83) DEC COLONIAE GLEV[ENSIS]
VIXIT AN LXXX QVI[NQVE]

161

A fragment from the middle of the tombstone of
'——— ———, *Councillor of the Colony of Glevum, who lived eighty-five years.*'

A LITTLE GIRL

84) D   M
SVCC · PETRONIAE · VIX
ANN·III·M·IIII·D·IX·VEP··O
MVΛVS · ET · VICTSABINA
FIΛ·KAR·FEC

164

This stone was complete at bottom, but the usual gable-shaped top, with the letters D·M, had probably been knocked off in order to fit the stone into the mediaeval walls.

'*To Successa Petronia, who lived three years, four months and nine days; Vep--omulus and Victoria Sabina set this up to their beloved daughter.*'

FIΛ·KAR·FEC = *filiae carissimae fecerunt.*

The Celtic name of the father was damaged before Leland saw the stone.

For the Greek K instead of C, cf. No. 109. In addition, the letter L is twice written Λ, as in Greek.

TWO SOLDIERS

85) IVLIVS · VITA
LIS · FABRICIES
IS·LEG·XX·V·V·
S T I P E N D I O R
VM·IX·ANOR·XX
IX · NATIONE · BE
LGA·EX·COLEGIO
FABRICE · ELATV
S · H S E

156

'*Julius Vitalis, Armourer in Legion XX Valeria Victrix, who served for nine years and lived for twenty-nine; a Belgian by race; buried, as a former member, by the Armourers' Club. He lies here.*'

FABRICE in line 8 is short for *Fabriciensium*. Vitalis was evidently one of the legionary armourers, who had formed a club or guild of the kind dear to craftsmen and even slaves under the Roman Empire. (Cf. No. 189.) Such clubs usually dined together at intervals, and paid their members' funeral expenses. People then as at other times were pathetically anxious to be remembered after death (it was the only immortality most of them hoped for) and morbidly interested in what became of their corpses.

Elatus: probably 'carried out (to burial)'.

86)   (Broken at top)

SER · · · · · · · INV S

NIC · EMERITVS · EX

LEG · XX · AN · XLV

H·S·E

G·TIBERINVS·HERES

F   C

160

'—— -inus, of the tribe Sergia, from Nicopolis, discharged from the Twentieth Legion, aged 45, lies here. Gaius Tiberinus his heir set up his stone.'

One of the several cities called Nicopolis is said by a historian to have had a Roman colony, of the tribe Sergia, planted in it; which Nicopolis we are not told.

§6   BRITAIN AND THE ROMAN OFFICIALS

Collingwood, following Haverfield, was fond of emphasising the thorough Romanisation of the Roman Empire, which made Roman Gaul or Roman Britain very different from British colonial India or Africa. He was particularly hard on Kipling, for picturing in *Puck of Pook's Hill* a Roman Britain conceived on British-Indian lines, with a sharp line between Romans and 'natives'. In this he was clearly right. With all their faults, the Romans never drew any such line; the absence of any great differences of colour from their Empire made this easier. Petillius

Cerialis, in the blunt 'Imperialist's Apology' that Tacitus[1] puts into his mouth when addressing the population of a town on the Rhine which he had just recaptured, in the rebellion of 69, reminds his hearers that Gauls might rise high in the Roman service and even command Roman armies. It was true. Julius Agricola himself, probably, from his name, of a family enfranchised by Julius Caesar, like Catullus and Vergil, from North Italy, may have had Celtic blood. Spain, first conquered and earliest Romanised of the western provinces, as early as the first century gave Rome a galaxy of clever writers—Lucan, the Senecas, Martial—and by A.D. 100 the emperor Trajan. Africa, the home of the Severi, the Gordians, Tertullian and St. Cyprian, reaches the same point a century and a half later. And in Britain, we have seen that the British workman spoke Latin and the British chieftain became a Roman squire living in a 'Roman villa'. The civilised Celt met the civilised Italian on equal terms, and made the same claim *Civis Romanus sum*. Martial, under Domitian, writes with admiration of a young lady who, though her ancestors were 'blue Britons', had married a Roman officer and was now being a social success at Rome.[2]

Still, this aspect of the Roman Empire can be exaggerated. It is certainly not true to say that there was *no* national feeling under the Empire. Juvenal, early in the second century, has a contemptuous snort for Greeks and Orientals, just as Cicero long before had described the Syrians as 'a nation born for slavery'. Claudius met with opposition when he first introduced Gauls into the Roman Senate. And Britain was a century younger as a Roman province than Gaul; it was remote, thinly populated, and damp; and from Derbyshire northward, so far from Romanisation being complete, the Brigantes in the second century broke out repeatedly into savage revolts. Juvenal speaks of 'storming Brigantian forts', when he wants a picturesque phrase to suggest a soldier's work on a distant frontier.[3]

The Romanisation of the small population of Britain, then, was something far more thorough and even different in kind from anything that Britain ever achieved in India. But yet it does remain true that to the average first or second century Roman civil servant or commissioned officer, Britain was still a

---

[1] *Histories*, iv, cc. 73-74.   [2] *Epigrams*, xi, No. 53.   [3] xiv, l. 196.

R.B.—F

remote subject territory to which he 'went out' to serve the state, and from which he returned thankfully to his home in the more congenial climate of Provence or Spain or Italy.

For the career of a Roman soldier of senatorial rank who rose to be governor of Britian, we need look no further than Tacitus' *Agricola*. Inscriptions, however, tell us something of other Roman officials, such as the procurators, of equestrian rank, who did anything from financial work to commanding the British fleet; or the important law officer, of senatorial rank, never mentioned by the historians, the *iuridicus Britanniae*, first appointed, it would seem, by Vespasian, as supreme judicial authority under the governor, at the time when Agricola was occupied all summer on his northern campaigns.

A JUDICIAL OFFICIAL

87) *C. Octavio Tidio Tossiano Iaoleno Prisco, l. leg. IV Flav., leg. leg. III Aug., iuridic. provinc. Brittaniae, leg. consulari provinc. Germ. superioris, legato consulari provinc. Syriae, proconsuli provinc. Africae, pontifici, P. Mutilius P. f. Cla. Crispinus t. p. i. amico carissimo.*

D 1015

'To *Gaius Octavius Tidius Tossianus Iaolenus Priscus, legate of the Fourth (Flavia) Legion, legate of the Third (Augusta) Legion, Law Officer of the Province of Britain, consular Governor of the Province of Upper Germany, consular Governor of the Province of Syria, Proconsul of the Province of Africa, Member of the College of Pontifices; Publius Mutilius Crispinus, son of Publius, of the tribe Claudia, bade this be set up under his will, to his good friend.*'

From Nadin in Dalmatia. Priscus was consul in 86, and must therefore have been in Britain before that; probably under Agricola. His long string of names is characteristic of the late first and early second century, at which period people added to their own names of people who had adopted them and left them property, of their maternal relatives, of a powerful friend or patron—accumulating names in fact as a feudal noble might accumulate quarterings.

Iavolenus, as he is elsewhere spelt, is known to students of Roman law as a jurist of some renown. He is also mentioned by Pliny (*Letters*, vi, 15), who was shocked at his raising a laugh by an interruption at a literary recitation.

T. p. i. = testamento poni iussit.

Crispinus seems to have economised by omitting mention of offices which Priscus must have held at Rome, including even the consulship; emphasising instead that he was (necessarily) of consular rank when he governed Syria and Upper Germany. Membership of one of the priestly *Collegia*, such as that of the Pontifices, of which the Emperor as Pontifex Maximus was head, was among the most *recherché* honours bestowed by the emperors upon leading senators.

A COMMANDER OF THE FLEET

88) *M. Maenio C. f. Cor. Agrippae L. Tusidio Campestri, hospiti divi Hadriani, patri senatoris, praef. coh. II. Fl. Britton. equitat., electo a divo Hadriano et misso in expeditionem Britannicam, trib. coh. I Hispanor. equitat., praef. alae Gallor. et Pannonior. catafractatae, proc. Aug. praef. classis Brittannicae, proc. provinciae Brittanniae, equo publico, patrono municipi, vicani Censorglacenses consecuti ab indulgentia optimi maximique imp. Antonini Aug. Pii beneficio interpretationis eius privilegia quibus in perpetuum aucti confirmatique sunt. L. d. d. d.*

D 2735

'To *Marcus Maenius Agrippa, son of Gaius, of the tribe Cornelia, (also named) Lucius Tusidius Campester, host of the late Emperor Hadrian, father of the Senator, Commandant of Vespasian's Own Second British part-mounted Battalion, picked by the Emperor Hadrian for active service in Britain, Tribune in command of the First Spanish part-mounted Battalion, Commandant of the Gallic and Pannonian Cuirassiers, Imperial Commissioner in command of the British Fleet, Finance Officer of the Province of Britain, Knight on the Establishment, Patron of this Township, the Villagers of Censorglacium, having through the favour of his mediation obtained by the kindness of His Imperial and Gracious Majesty Antoninus Augustus Pius the privileges in whose enjoyment they are permanently confirmed, (dedicate this memorial) on ground given by decree of the Parish Council.'*

From Camerini in Italy; the village of Censorglacium (or the like) is not otherwise known. The people of a backward hill district proudly erect a memorial to their first distinguished citizen, who has gone far in the imperial service, and is the father of a son who, having reached the Senate, is in a fair way to go further still; and incidentally the man whose influence has won for them certain *privilegia*, probably the character of a corporate *vicus* or 'civil parish'.

Maenius Agrippa, who thus commanded Britons or served in Britain in no less than four of his appointments, bears another accumulation of names.

Coh. II. Fl., etc.—i.e., Flavia, the family name of Vespasian and his sons. This cohort was serving on the lower Danube in 99.

On Hadrian's *expeditio Britannica*, see below, Nos. 96ff.

The Coh. I Hisp. was stationed in Britain (see next inscr.); the Gallo-Pannonian Cuirassiers, again on the Danube.

The Procurator of the Province (thus distinguished from all the lesser procurators of Britain) would be the chief financial official.

The Romans never finally decided how many t's and n's there were in 'Britain' and spellings vary; this inscription and the last give a complete set of variants.

Equo Publico: In primitive Rome it had been the duty of every citizen possessing a certain amount of property to serve, if called upon, in the city's cavalry. Later a distinction was drawn between the members of the eighteen ancient centuries of *Equites Equo Publico*, whose horses were found by the State, and additional cavalrymen who found their own—*equites equo privato*. With the growth of a professional army the class naturally ceased to have anything to do with military matters, and under the law of Gaius Gracchus, of 122 B.C., it was officially defined as including all citizens possessed of not less than 400,000 sesterces (100,000 times the day's pay for a labourer). Under Augustus, thousands of prosperous tradesmen were thus included in the *equester ordo*, many of them being people of ignoble or foreign origin, sometimes even freedmen; so Augustus, who was nothing if not class-conscious, revived the old Eighteen Centuries of *Equites Equo Publico* (henceforth also known as *equites illustres* or *splendidi*), inclusion on whose roll was a real distinction, conferred by the Emperor, as successor of the old censors. The only duty which it involved was presence, if within reach, at a brilliant annual quasi-military parade at which the Emperor reviewed the Centuries just as the old republican Censors had reviewed their predecessors.

L. d. d. d. = *loco dato decreto decurionum*.

MAENIUS IN CUMBERLAND

As Tribune of the 1st Spaniards, Maenius was stationed at Alauna, now Ellenborough near Maryport, on the coast of Cumberland, and four altars dedicated by him and his unit have been found there, of which one may be quoted:

89)

I · O · M

COH·I·HIS

CVI PRAE

M · MAENI

VS· AGRIP

TRIBV

POS

823

'*To Jupiter the Best and Greatest, the 1st Spanish Cohort, under Marcus Maenius Agrippa, Tribune, dedicate this.*'

(Expanded version of the Latin: *Iovi Optimo Maximo Cohors Prima Hispanorum, cui praeest M. Maenius Agrippa tribunus, posuit.*)

CAMULODUNUM

90) *Gn. Munatius M. f. Pal. Aurelius Bassus proc. Aug., praef. fabr., praef. coh. III sagittariorum, praef. coh. iterum II Asturum, censitor civium Romanorum coloniae Victricensis quae est in Brittannia Camaloduni, curator viae Nomentanae, patronus eiusdem municipi, flamen perpetuus, duumvirali potestate aedilis, dictator IIII.*
CIL XIV, 3955

Near Nomentum in Latium; tombstone recording the career of an equestrian officer, evidently a great man in the little decayed Latin town that was his home. Dictator, the title of an emergency officer at Rome, was that of the ordinary annual chief magistrate at several of the ancient Italian towns. Aediles, at Nomentum, as at Rome, are the junior magistrates who looked after the municipal buildings and policed the streets.

'*Gnaeus Munatius Aurelius Bassus, son of Marcus, of the tribe Palatina, Imperial Procurator, Officer of Engineers, Commandant of the 3rd Archers, again Commandant of the 2nd Asturian Cohort, Census Officer for the Roman citizens of the Colony of Victory at Camalodunum in Britain, Curator of the Nomentum Road and Patron of the township,*

Priest for life, Aedile, entrusted with magisterial power, four times Dictator.'

Munatius thus serves at least twice in Britain, his first post here being the command of the 2nd Asturians (cf. No. 23), who have left their mark in Wales.

THE LONG ROADS

91)
>
> D E O · QVI · VIAS
> ET · SEMITAS. COM
> MENTVS · EST · T · IR
> DAS·S·C·F·V·L·L·M
> Q·VARIVS·VITA
> LIS BF COS ARAM
> SACRAM   RESTI
> TVIT
> APRONIANO·ET·BRA
> DUA COS

725

From Catterick Bridge over the River Swale.

'To the God who thought up roads and trails, Titus Irdas(?), of the Governor's Bodyguard, gladly, willingly and duly did his vow.

Quintus Varius Vitalis, of the Governor's Staff, restored this holy altar in the consulship of Apronianus and Bradua.'

Discovered in 1620, and since lost; printed from a copy by Camden. The name Irdas is strange, perhaps corrupt.

S.C.F.V.L.L.M. = *Singularis Consularis* (one of the 'hand-picked' men in attendance on the consular governor) *fecit* (for more usual *solvit) votum laetus libens merito*; BF COS, *beneficiarius consularis*, cf. No. 174, etc.

Deo to *est* can be scanned as an iambic line (with *vias* as one syllable); the unusual dedication might be a line from a play. But anyone who has travelled over rough country with no path at all will appreciate the point. Both the original dedicator and the restorer are Headquarters men, whose lot, like that of the Governor himself, would include riding the length of England repeatedly.

Apronianus and Bradua were consuls in 191. The altar then needing repair may well have been a hundred years old already.

CHAPTER III

THE NORTHERN WARS AND ROMAN SCOTLAND
(*c.* A.D. 85-185)

§1   THE NORTH AFTER AGRICOLA

Agricola handed over his province to his successor, says Tacitus, peaceful and secure (*Agr.* 40). He had broken the last formed opposition, probably near the Moray Firth; his fleet had sailed round the north and made unopposed landings even in the Orkneys. It was not unreasonable for his son-in-law to complain that 'Britain was completely conquered and then forthwith let go' (*Histories*, i, 2).

The trouble was that the government (Domitian's) needed troops elsewhere, especially when the Dacians twice defeated his generals on the Danube. It seemed that they might now safely be taken from Britain. Leg. II Adiutrix was on the Danube in time to win decorations in Domitian's Dacian War, which was over by A.D. 90:

92)   *T.Cominius T.f. Volt. Severus Vienna, Ɔ Leg.II Adiutric., donis donato ab imp. Caesare Aug. bello Dacico torquibus armillis phaleris corona vallari vixit ann. xxxxv. T. Caesernius Macedo proc. Aug. her. ex test. posuit.*

D. 9193, from Sirmium, on the Save, west of Belgrade.

'*T. Cominius Severus, son of Titus, of the tribe Voltinia, from Vienne, Centurion in Leg.II Adiutrix, decorated by His Majesty in the Dacian War with neck-chains, armlets, medals and the crown for storming a stockade, lived for 45 years. T. Caesernius Macedo, Imperial Procurator, his heir, set up this monument under his will.*'

Vienna = Vienne on the Rhone (our Vienna, Wien, was Vindobona).

Which emperor it was is shown by the *absence* of his name. After Domitian's murder and *damnatio memoriae*, persons honoured by him hung on to their honours, but avoided mentioning their source so far as possible!

No doubt some *auxilia* left Britain with the legion. The army left there was awkwardly extended, and it was decided to shorten the line in the north.

This is why the great legionary fortress at Inchtuthil on the Tay, planned by Agricola, was never completely finished. Five coins, datable about 86 and in mint condition when lost, found by Richmond on the site, date the excavation with some accuracy. The huge squared timbers, lately erected to form the corners of gate-towers, were eased out of their holes, squeezing down the earth on the downward side in the process, and no doubt lashed together in rafts to be floated away south for re-use. Everything possible was removed or 'denied to the enemy'. A large mass of iron nails, ranging from small tacks to huge 12-inch spikes, still left when the last convoy was going, was buried—to be found in 1961 in remarkably good condition, the outside alone having rusted, and protected the remainder. XX Legion was ordered back for the winter to the vacant base at Chester, and from the way in which they dealt with surplus Samian crockery—pulverising it with hammers and using the results to block the drains which they had lately dug—it would appear that they were very angry indeed.

The Twentieth Legion at Chester

93)

      C . LOVESIVS · PAPIR
      CADARVS · EMERITA · MIL
      LEG·XX·V·V·ANN·XXV·STIP·IIX

501   FRONTINVS AQVILO · H · F · C ·

'*Gaius Lovesius Cadarus, of the tribe Papiria, (born at) Emerita; soldier in Legion XX Valeria Victrix; (died aged) 25 years, after eight years' service. Frontinus Aquilo his heir set this up.*'

Emerita is Merida in Spain, a very great city under the Roman Empire. Augustus settled there a colony of his time-expired soldiers, after the Civil Wars—whence its full name, Emerita Augusta. Lovesius Cadarus' two names are native Spanish. He seems to have joined the army at 17. For a still more surprising case of a boy soldier, cf. No. 29.

94)

D   M

CAECILIVS·AVIT

VS·EMER· AVG ·

OPTIO · LEG · XX ·

V·V·STP·XV·VIX·

ANN · XXXIIII ·

H   ·   F   ·   C

492

'(*Dis Manibus.*) *Caecilius Avitus, of Emerita, Sergeant in Legion XX Valeria Victrix, served for 15 years and lived for 34. His heir set this up.*'

An Optio was the second-in-command of a century, the understudy of a centurion (cf. No. 38).

Therewith, the far-flung forts that still guarded Strathmore, up to Rome's furthest fort of all at Stracathro, facing the Mounth and the jaws of Glenesk, had to be given up too. The front line came back to the Isthmus, with perhaps an outpost, heavily fortified, at Ardoch on Allan Water, another Alauna. Meanwhile southern Scotland was still strongly held, many of Agricola's forts being rebuilt, sometimes replaced by larger ones, as at Dalswinton in Nithsdale and (largest of all) at the focal point of Newstead-by-Melrose on the Tweed; Trimontium as the Romans called it, from the three peaks of the Eildon Hills, conspicuous to troops coming over the Cheviots by Dere Street, above Carter Bar.

There was a considerable saving of manpower. But the enemy were encouraged. Juvenal (iv, 127) speaks of a chariot-driving British king, Arviragus, as among Rome's chief enemies under Domitian (Shakespeare took up his name, to give to a Briton in *Cymbeline*); and early in Trajan's reign there are signs of a serious rebellion, with destruction at Newstead and as far south as Agricola's fort at Corbridge on the Tyne. It took a considerable campaign to restore the position, as shown by a distinct occupation-stratum at several forts in southern Scotland.

MILITARY DIPLOMAS

All this coming and going is not illustrated by a single inscription. Inscriptions in Scotland are found in quantity only at sites re-occupied in the mid-second century, though one or two tombstones (Nos. 37, 176?) may be earlier. But it is now that we begin to have considerable light shed on the army-list of the *auxilia* in Britain by the useful documents known as Military Diplomas (cf. Nos. 36, 71, from the continent).

When a soldier in the auxilia was honourably discharged after his twenty-five years' service he received Roman citizenship; this was one of the chief methods by which citizenship was extended, until by the famous edict of 211 it was possessed by all free subjects of the Emperor. An imperial edict was from time to time issued, naming all the auxiliary regiments in a small province, or *some* of those in a large army like that of Britain (perhaps those attached to one or more legions) announcing the grant of discharge and citizenship. It was engraved on bronze and affixed to a wall at Rome, first on the Capitol, and later, when the available walls and monuments there were completely covered, on the Palatine. These records have long since been melted down; but a discharged auxiliary soldier might have a copy made, as a certificate of his citizenship and the legitimacy in Roman law of his children; and many of these have been discovered.

By a law of Nero (Suetonius, *Nero*, 17), any document that was to be legally binding had to be made out in duplicate on both sides of a tablet, which was then folded (by means of a hinge, if the tablet was of rigid material), tied up with three threads, passing through holes in both halves of the tablet, and sealed by witnesses, on the thread, the witnesses' names being written opposite the seal. The seals were only broken and the writing within inspected, to see if it corresponded to that without, by a competent authority and in case of necessity. (This is why, in the *Apocalypse of St. John* (ch. v), much is made of finding 'One worthy' to 'loose the seven seals' of the Book of Life. It is ironic that this Christian picture of the certificate to end all certificates should conceive it in the form of a Neronian legal document.)

Hence the name 'diplomas', i.e. folded documents, commonly applied to these auxiliary soldiers' discharge-certificates.

Their interest for us lies in the fact that though only one soldier's name is given, that of the owner, the imperial edict is given in full, including the list of regiments. Several diplomas from one province will give something like a complete list;

especially since the Romans, without mechanical transport, frequently left a regiment in one province for centuries, and never moved one without very good reason.

Seven datable diplomas referring to Britain are known; of A.D. 98 (a fragment), 103, 105, 122, 124, 135 and 146. That of 103, a fine specimen in good condition, found at Malpas, Cheshire, is worth quoting:

95) *Imp. Caesar divi Nervae f. Nerva Traianus Augustus Germanicus Dacicus, pontifex maximus, tribunic. potestat VII, imp. IIII, p. p., cos. V, equitibus et peditibus, qui militant in alis quattuor et cohortibus decem et una quae appellantur I Thracum et I Pannoniorum Tampiana et Gallorum Sebosiana et Hispanorum Vettonum C. R., et I Hispanorum et I Vangionum milliaria et I Alpinorum et I Morinorum et I Cugernorum et I Baetasiorum et I Tungrorum et I Thracum et III Bracaraugustanorum et IIII Lingonum et IIII Delmatarum, et sunt in Britannia sub L. Neratio Marcello, qui quina et vicena plurave stipendia meruerunt, quorum nomina subscripta sunt: ipsis liberis posterisque eorum civitatem dedit et conubium cum uxoribus quas tunc habuissent cum est civitas iis data, aut si qui caelibes essent, cum iis quas postea duxissent dumtaxat singuli singulas.*

A. d. XIIII Kal. Febr. M'. Laberio Maximo II, Q. Glitio Agricola II cos.

Alae I Pannoniorum Tampianae, cui praest C. Valerius Celsus, decurioni: Reburro Severi f., Hispan. Descriptum et recognitum ex tabula aenea, quae fixa est Romae in muro post templum divi Aug. ad Minervam.

[*Witness the seals of:*]

Q. Pompei Homeri	*C. Papi Eusebetis*
T. Flavi Secundi	*P. Cauli Vitalis*
C. Vettieni Modesti	*P. Atini Hedonici*
	Ti. Claudi Menandri

CIL XVI, 48
D 2001

A few notes, bracketed [ ], are given in the translation:

'*The Emperor Caesar, son of the deified Nerva, Nerva Traianus Augustus Germanicus Dacicus, Head of the Sacred College, in the seventh year of his reign, four times hailed Imperator, Father of his Country, five times Consul,*

To the cavalry and infantry soldiers serving in the four alae *and eleven cohorts which are called—*

[Cavalry]
1st Thracian
Tampius' 1st Pannonian
Sebosius' Gauls [one of the Gallic *alae* with no numbers]
Vettonian Spaniards, Roman citizens [From Portugal]

[Infantry]
1st Spaniards
1st Vangiones, 1000 strong [From the Rhineland]
1st Alpine
1st Morini [Near Boulogne. Their name means "sea-folk".]
1st Cugerni [Rhineland]
1st Baetasii [Rhineland]
1st Tungri [Belgium—modern Tongres. Mentioned by Tacitus at M. Craupius]
1st Thracians
3rd Bracarians [From Bracara Augusta—modern Braga—Portugal]
4th Lingones [Modern Langres, France]
4th Dalmatians
—and who are now in Britain under Lucius Neratius Marcellus, and have served not less than twenty-five years, and whose names appear below,

Has granted citizenship, for themselves, their Children and their posterity, and Rights of Marriage with the wives whom they had when citizenship was granted to them, or in the case of unmarried men with those whom they may afterwards have married; but not more than one wife to one man.

[*Dated*] *January 19, in the Second Consulship of Manius Laberius Maximus, and the Second of Quintus Glitius Agricola.* [=A.D. 103.]

[*This copy belongs*] *to Reburrus, son of Severus, the Spaniard, Troop-Leader in Tampius' First Pannonian Cavalry—Commanding Officer, Gaius Valerius Celsus.*

Copied from and compared with the bronze tablet affixed at Rome to the wall behind the Temple of the deified Augustus near the Temple of Minerva.

Witnessed by ——' *etc.*

That this troop-leader in the First Pannonian Cavalry comes from a different province is in no way unusual.

The Governor, Neratius Marcellus, is known to us also from Pliny's Letters. Pliny, in the normal way of patronage, obtained from him the offer of a commission for Suetonius, later the biographer of emperors; but Suetonius, mightier with the pen than the sword, gracefully declined it and asked if he might pass it on to another friend.

The diplomas of 98 and 105, both much damaged, enable us to add to the list another four cavalry *alae* and eleven cohorts; indeed, they do not overlap much, referring probably to groups under different legionary commands. It is not likely that we have as yet anything like the full 'order of battle' for this period.

§2 THE CRISIS OF 117 AND THE MYSTERY OF THE NINTH LEGION

In any case the army in Britain proved to be not large enough; for at the end of Trajan's reign (117) there was a disaster. The Romans lost everything north of the Solway and Tyne. It has been customary to associate this with the disappearance of Leg. IX Hispana from the army list.

The last dated evidence of this legion in Britain is the building-inscription of 108 from York, No. 41 above; and by 122 Leg. VI Victrix had arrived in Britain to replace it. It was inferred that the Ninth had been destroyed, and not merely suffered heavy casualties but been disgraced and cashiered, as part of the disaster that lost southern Scotland

But there are difficulties. Ritterling pointed out long ago that there were at least two officers still in the middle of their careers over twenty years later, who had served in the Ninth, and who would have been very old for the posts they were then holding, if such service had to be before 120 (Dessau, *ILS* 1070, 1077, which it would require too much space to cite in full.) Theories have been developed to account for the absence of any mention of the Ninth among the numerous building-inscriptions of Hadrians' Wall (*c.* 122) by supposing that it was then in Scotland, 'keeping the outfield', or in the western sector, where for lack of stone the wall was built of turf and inscriptions were on wood (one small fragment has survived). But a new turn was given to the debate by the recent discovery at Nijmegen on the lower Rhine, where again stone for inscriptions was lacking, of a tile and a *mortarium* bearing the stamp of LEGIO VIIII. The context is Hadrianic. The debate is not closed, but it seems most likely that, perhaps when Trajan was shifting troops eastward for his Parthian war, the Ninth was moved to the continent, and that it disgraced itself and was disbanded in some later disaster, such as the Jewish War of Bar-Cochba, after 132. The prelude to the loss of Scotland was then the reduction of the army of Britain to only two legions.

THE SIXTH LEGION AT TYNEMOUTH

The arrival of Legion VI from Castra Vetera on the lower Rhine is signalled by the inscriptions on two fine altars found in the Tyne at Newcastle. These also make it probable that it was brought direct to Tynemouth by sea; straight to the war area, where it could cut through by Agricola's road, 'The Stanegate', from Newcastle to Carlisle, between the rebels in Northumbria and Scotland.

Both altars are perfectly unweathered and 'as new'. It looks as though they were dedicated to the sea-gods, when the great convoy safely arrived in the Tyne, by the simple method of sinking them—where they were found, deep in the mud, when the foundations of the Swing Bridge were being laid.

96)

NEPTVNO·LE

VI   VI

P   F

(Central decoration:
a dolphin and a trident)

1319

97)

OCIANO·LEG

VI   VI

P   F

(Central decoration:
an anchor)

1320

'*To Neptune, Legion VI Victrix, Pia Fidelis.*'
'*To Ocean, Legion VI Victrix, Pia Fidelis.*'
OCIANO = *Oceano*; cf. *aginte* for *agente* in No. 21.
VI VI = *Sexta, Victrix*; PF = *Pia Fidelis*, 'Loyal and True'.

FURTHER REINFORCEMENTS

In addition to the Sixth Legion and thousands of auxiliaries, horse and foot, three thousand other legionaries from Spain and Upper Germany were sent over, as we see from an inscription in Italy, recording the unusual career of the veteran soldier under whom they were brigaded.

98)   *T. Pontius T. f. Pal. Sabinus, praef. coh. I Pann. et Dalmat. eq. c. R., trib. mil. leg. VI Ferrat., donis donatus expeditione Parthica a divo Traiano hasta pura vexillo corona murali, › leg. XXII Primig., › leg. XIII Gemin., primus pilus leg. III Aug., praepositus vexillationibus milliariis tribus expeditione Brittannica, leg. VII Gemin. VIII Aug. XXII Primig., trib. coh. III vig., coh. XIIII urb., coh. II praet., p. p. II, proc. provinc. Narbonens., IIII vir i. d. quinq., flamen, patron. municipi.*

D 2726; from Ferentinum in Latium

'*Titus Pontius Sabinus, son of Titus, of the tribe Palatina, Commandant of the First Pannonian and Dalmatian Cohort, part-mounted, Roman Citizens; Military Tribune in Legion VI Ferrata; presented by his late Majesty the Emperor Trajan in the Parthian expedition with the decorations of the Silver Spear, Standard, and Mural Crown; Centurion in Legion XXII Primigenia; Centurion in Legion XIII Gemina; Chief Centurion in Legion III Augusta; Officer Commanding the three detachments of one thousand men from Legions VII Gemina, VIII Augusta, XXII Primigenia, in the British campaign; Tribune of the Third Cohort of Police; of the Fourteenth Urban Cohort; of the Second Cohort of the Guard; Senior Centurion a second time; Procurator of the Provinc dae Gallia Narbonensis; Municipal Magistrate in the census-year, Priest nof Patron of this Corporate Town.*'

Legion VI Ferrata—'the Ironsides'—lay in Syria; it will be while serving in it that Pontius receives the decorations customary for a Tribune.

Legion XXII Primig. served, as we have seen, in Germany, XIII Gemina in newly conquered Dacia, III Aug. in Africa—the imposing ruins of Timgad are the remains of its work. VIII Augusta lay in Upper Germany, VII Gemina in Spain.

Pontius' career is an odd one. It looks—as it looked first to Mommsen—as if, after serving in the first two posts of a normal equestrian career, he found immediate prospects of promotion not very promising and decided to step down one grade and accept an immediate commission as centurion. In this he did very well, holding the *locuples aquila* of Juvenal (*Sat.* xiv) twice, returning to 'field officer' rank among the metropolitan troops (cf. No. 16) and ending with one of the best Procuratorships.

IIII vir i. d. quinq. = *quattuorvir iuris dicendi quinquennalis*, '*Member of the Board of Four Judicial Magistrates in the Fifth Year.*' The chief executive officers of a Roman corporate town were regularly four in number—sometimes divided into a senior pair, the *duoviri*, who transacted judicial and administrative business, and a junior, the *aediles* (cf. No. 90). Those of the census-year, one year in five, were of particular importance, as they had to collect *inter alia* the property returns on which taxation was based for the next quinquennium.

A Shield from the Tyne

It is likely that these detachments, like Legion VI, sailed direct to the Tyne. At least one relic of their presence was found in that river. It is an ornamental metal centre-piece, for attachment to the iron-bound board-and-canvas legionary shield, adorned in niello with an eagle, with Mars and a bull (the crest of the Eighth Legion) above and below, and, in the four corners, figures representing the Seasons. The owner had stippled it carefully with his name and 'address':

99)   IVNI DVBITATI
                  Ↄ IVL MAGNI LEG VIII AVG

BM, p. 77f

'*Junius Dubitatus; Julius Magnus' Century, Leg. VIII Augusta.*' Poor Junius.

The Auxilia under Hadrian

The general whom Hadrian sent to cope with the crisis was Q. Pompeius Falco, one of Trajan's right-hand men, who had commanded a legion in Dacia, governed Judaea, now garrisoned by the Tenth Legion, and now came straight from the responsible command south of the lower Danube. His career may be studied in *D* 1035. He was another polyonymous nobleman, a friend of Pliny, and married to a grand-daughter of S. Julius Frontinus, thrice consul and sometime governor of Britain. His name figures in the finest of all our Military Diplomas, which by chance belonged to a soldier in the same regiment as Reburrus, the troop-commander discharged in 103. The huge list of regiments, unparalleled in any other known diploma, is presumably a complete list of those in Falco's northern army, about three-quarters of all those in Britain; some must still have been left in the south, under command of the Legate of II Augusta.

The soldier named is a Pannonian lance-corporal ('one-and-a-half-pay-man') in the Pannonian cavalry, and unlike Reburrus, who presumably settled in Cheshire where his tablet was found, he went home. His certificate was found in 1930 at O-Szöny on the Danube in western Hungary, Roman Brigetio, and acquired by the British Museum.

By this time most of the old Spanish and southern Gallic cohorts and *alae* were being recruited from other peoples; the old sources were drying up, partly because so many families had acquired Roman citizenship and their sons could serve in the legions; but Rhineland and Danubian peoples continued to recruit both their own and other regiments. This is the prelude to the situation in the third century, when the army of Illyricum (the Danube lands) dominated the empire and provided a series of great soldier emperors.

100) IMP CAESAR DIVI TRAIANI PARTHICI F DIVI NERVAE NEPOS TRA
IANVS HADRIANVS AVGVSTVS PONTIFEX MAXIMVS TRIBV
NIC POTESTAT · VI · COS · III · PROCOS
EQVITIB ET PEDITIB QVI MILITAVERVNT IN ALIS DECEM ET TRIB ET COH
TIB TRIGINTA ET SEPTEM QVAE APPELLANTVR I PANNONIOR SABINIAN
ET I PANNON TAMPIAN ET I HISPAN ASTVR ET I TVNGROR ET II ASTVR
ET GALLOR PICENTIAN ET GALLOR ET THRAC CLASSIANA CR ET GALLOR
PETRIANA ∞ CR ET GALLOR SEBOSIANA ET VETTON HISPAN CR ET
AGRIPPIANA MINIATA ET AVG GALLOR ET AVG VOCONTIOR CR ET I
NERVIA GERMAN CR ET I CELTIBEROR ET I THRAC ET I AFROR CR ET I
LINGON ET I FID VARDVLLOR ∞ CR ET I FRISIAVON ET I VANGION
∞ ET I HAMIOR SAGITT ET I DELMAT ET I AQVITAN ET I VLPIA TRAIA
NA CVGERN CR ET I MORIN ET I MENAPIOR ET I SVNVCOR ET I BETA
SIOR ET I BATAVOR ET I TVNGROR ET I HISPAN ET II GALLOR ET II
VASCON CR ET II THRAC ET II LINGON ET II ASTVR ET II DELMATAR
ET II NERVIOR ET III NERVIOR ET III BRACAROR ET III LINGON

o   o

ET IV GALLOR ET IV BREVCOR ET IV DELMATAR ET V RAETOR
ET V GALLOR ET VI NERVIOR ET VII THRAC QVAE SVNT IN BRITAN
R.B.—G

NIA SVB A PLATORIO NEPOTE QVINQVE ET VIGINTI STIPENDIS
EMERITIS DIMISSIS HONESTA MISSIONE PER POMPEIVM
FALCONEM · QVORM · NOMINA SVBSCRIPTA SVNT IPSIS LIBE
RIS POSTERISQ EORVM CIVITATEM DEDIT ET CONVB CVM VXO
RIB QVAS TVNC HABVISSENT CVM EST CIVITAS IIS DATA
AVT SI QVI CAELIBES ESSENT CVM IIS QVAS POSTEA DVXIS
SENT DVMTAXAT SINGVLI SINGVLAS AD XVI K AVG
TI IVLIO CAPITON ET L VITRASIO FLAMININO COS

ALAE I PANNONIOR TAMPIANAE   CVI PRAEST
    FABIVS   SABINVS
   EX SESQVIPLICARIO
   GEMELLO BREVCI F PANNON
DESCRIPTVM ET RECOGNITVM · EX · TABVLA · AENEA QVAE FIXA EST
ROMAE IN MVRO POST TEMPLVM DIVI AVG AD MINERVAM

TI·CLAVDI		MENANDRI
A·FVLVI	O	IVSTI
TI·IVLI		VRBANI
L·PVLLI		DAPHNI
L·NONI	O	VICTORIS
Q·LOLLI		FEST[I
L·PULLI		ANT[

CIL XVI, 65

In the following annotated translation, regiments that have appeared in No. 95, above, are indicated by that number.

'*The Emperor Caesar, son of the deified Trajan, Conqueror of Parthia, grandson of the deified Nerva, Traianus Hadrianus Augustus, Pontifex Maximus, in the sixth year of his reign, thrice Consul, Proconsul,*

To the cavalry and infantry soldiers who have served in the thirteen cavalry regiments and thirty-seven cohorts named as follows,

1st Pannonians (Sabinus' Horse)
1st Pannonians (Tampius' Horse) [95]
1st Spanish Asturians
1st Tungrians [95]
2nd Asturians
Gauls (Picentius' Horse)
Gauls and Thracians (Classicus' Horse) [product of a recent amalgamation?]
Gauls (Petreius' Horse), 1000 strong, Roman Citizens [an honour recently won]
Gauls (Sebosius' Horse) [95]

Vettonian Spaniards, Roman Citizens [95]
Agrippa's Horse, Miniata [meaning not known]
Augustus' Own Gauls
Augustus' Own Vocontii, Roman Citizens [from Provence originally]
[The cavalry end here]
1st Nerva's Own Germans, Roman Citizens
1st Celtiberians
1st Thracians [95]
1st Africans, Roman Citizens [from Tunisia]
1st Lingones [Langres, eastern France]
1st Loyal Vardullians, 1000 strong, Roman Citizens [from Spain]
1st Frisians [from north-west Holland]
1st Vangiones, 1000 strong (95)
1st Hamian Archers [from Hamah, Biblical Hamath, Syria; the only oriental regiment]
1st Dalmatians
1st Aquitanians [from the mediaeval Aquitaine]
1st Trajan's Own Cugerni, Roman Citizens [95; with a new title of honour]
1st Morini [95]
1st Menapii [neighbours of the Morini at home]
1st Sunuci [Rhinelanders]
1st Baetasii [95]
1st Batavi [from Holland; the last in Britain of Agricola's Batavi]
1st Tungri [95]
1st Spaniards [95]
2nd Gauls [i.e. from Central Gaul; northern or Belgic Gallic regiments bear their tribal names]
2nd Basques [from N.E. Spain]
2nd Lingones
2nd Asturians
2nd Dalmatians
2nd Nervii [from the Ardennes; the tribe that nearly beat Caesar]
3rd Nervii
3rd Bracarians [95]
3rd Lingones
4th Gauls

4th Lingones [95; omitted by the copyist in the text above, but
given on the other side of the tablet]
4th Breuci
4th Dalmatians [95]
5th Raeti [or Rhaeti; between the Alps and the upper Danube]
5th Gauls
6th Nervii
7th Thracians

*which are in Britain under Aulus Platorius Nepos, who have served
twenty-five years and have received their honourable discharge from
Pompeius Falco, whose names appear below,*

   *To them, their children and their posterity, has Granted Citizenship and
lawful marriage with the wives that they had at the time of the grant of
citizenship, or, in the case of unmarried men, with those whom they may
marry hereafter, but not more than one wife to one man*

This 16th day before the Kalends of August [*July 17th*]
in the Consulship of Tiberius Julius Capito [A.D. *122*]
      and Lucius Vitrasius Flamininus

1st Pannonian Cavalry (*Tampius' Horse*) *commanded by*
      Fabius Sabinus
      To ex-Lance-Corporal
      Gemellus, son of Breucus, Pannonian

*Copied and checked from the bronze tablet set up at Rome on the wall
behind the Temple of the deified Augustus near the Temple of Minerva.'*

The predominance of low serial numbers is due to the Roman
habit, whenever a new group of regiments was raised, of starting
again at I. Hence the army contained numerous First, Second and
Third Legions, and dozens of First Cohorts and *Alae* of the
various warlike nationalities. Serial numbers higher than III are
quite rare, being found only when several regiments of the same
nation have been raised together. Two 'First Alpine' Cohorts,
without distinguishing titles, actually appear serving together in
Pannonia!

   Among the witnesses, we notice that Tiberius Claudius
Menander, who has been affixing his seal to legal documents, no
doubt for a consideration, for 20 years since No. 95, has gradually
risen from last to first position.

The veterans of Pompeius Falco's great army (50,000 men including the legionaries) have been given their *honesta missio* by him, but before all the formalities have been completed and the tablets have been received from Rome, he has handed over to the new governor (122-6?), Hadrian's personal friend Platorius Nepos who superintended the building of the famous Wall. Hadrian himself came over, probably in 122, and personally reconnoitred the whole line of it, on foot, from sea to sea.

§3   THE BUILDING OF HADRIAN'S WALL

All along the line of the wall are found building-inscriptions of the usual types—ranging from the elaborate slabs set up by the headquarters of a legion to the roughly-cut work of a company under a centurion. Here are a few:

101)

IMP·CAES·TRAIAN

HADRIANI· AVG

LEG·II·AVG

A·PLATORIO·NEPOTE·LEG·PR·PR

1637, 1638

Discovered in 1725 and 1751, in the central portion of the wall.

'*The Emperor Caesar Traianus Hadrianus Augustus' Second (Augusta) Legion [built this], when Aulus Platorius Nepos was governor of Britain.*'

It was these stones which first made it quite certain by whom the stone wall was built. The early mediaeval Welshman, Gildas, and the Northumbrian, Bede, attributed it to the last days of Roman Britain; and the prevailing theory used to be that the builder was Severus, about 200—who did in fact repair and reorganise the defences, as many inscriptions show. Many fragments of similar stones of all the three legions have been found on the Wall.

Another fine stone, though much broken, found in 1937 at Benwell on the Tyne, commemorates the work of a landing party from the fleet:

102)

IMP   CAES   TRAIANO

HADR[IA]N   AVG

A PLATORIO N[EPOTE L]EG AVG PR PR

VEXILLATIO   C[LASSIS]   BRITAN

1340

'For the Emperor Caesar Traianus Hadrianus Augustus, a detachment of the British fleet (built this) under Aulus Platorius Nepos, Imperial Governor.'

103)

LEG XX VV

CHO IIII

Ɔ · LIB FRO

Ɔ TERE MAG

2077

'Legion XX Valeria Victrix, Cohort IV: Century of Liberius Fronto; Century of Terentius Magnus.'

From Newburn, not far west of Newcastle. The stone is elaborately decorated; to the right of the inscription is a standard, to the left a *vexillum* or detachment flag with the lettering LEG XX, and below, an eagle.

From Birdoswald, twelve miles from Carlisle, comes a less elaborate stone:

104)

LEG · VI

VIC·P·F

F

1916

'Legion VI Victrix Pia Fidelis built this.'
P·F·F = *Pia Fidelis fecit.*

Two stones commemorating auxiliary cohorts:

105)

COH I · TH

RACVM

1323

'First Thracian Cohort.'

From Newcastle. The letters are framed in a panel, with a roughly-sculptured palm-branch below and to the right.

106)

COH I BATA

VORVM · F

1823

'First Batavian Cohort built this.'

From Carvoran, the next station east of Birdoswald.

Three 'centurial stones':

107)   ⟩ CLAVDI

                                  P XXX SE

1813

'Claudius' Century; 30½ yards' (or *feet*).

From Carvoran.   SE = *semis*, 'half'; P, either *pedes* or *passus*.

108)   COH IIII ⟩ CLA

                                  C L E O N I C I

1648

'Fourth Cohort; Century of Claudius Cleonicus.'

From near Housesteads.   The centurion or his ancestors come from the Greek east.

109)   ⟩ KALPVR

                                  N I A N I

1655

'Century of Calpurnianus.'

From the central part of the wall; now in the Chesters Museum.

Some stones, very roughly cut, testify to the work of levies from the south of Britain and may commemorate rebuilding in later crises:

110)   C I V I T A T E C A T

                       V V E L L A V N

                       O R V M   ·   TOSS

                       [O] D I O

1962

'From the tribe of the Catuvellauni Tossodio(?) (built this)'

Built into the wall of an outhouse at Howgill, west of Birdoswald. *Tossodio* is perhaps a personal name.

111)   C I V I T A S

                       D V M N O N I

1844   In an outhouse near Carvoran:

'Canton of the Dumnonii' (the extreme south-western tribe—cf. modern 'Devon') in a rough panel. Another from the same district reads:

112)   C I V I T A S
                        D V M N I

1843; and two from near Housesteads (1671, 1672) similarly
commemorate work of the Durotriges of Dorset and Somerset.

Changes of Plan

Pure archaeology, independently of inscriptions, has unfolded
quite a dramatic story of changes of plan while the Wall was still
being built. The northern tribes, seeing the Romans withdraw and
'dig in', apparently on the defensive, were not content like
Dogberry to 'thank God they were rid of a knave'. They followed
up; and not only the Selgovae of the southern Scottish uplands,
but northerners. Actually a broch, one of those remarkable
towers characteristic of the northern highlands and islands, was
built on the edge of the ditches of Agricola's fort at Torwoodlee
in Selkirk, and Roman rubbish has been found under its foundations. And it looks as if this hostile movement developed early;
for within Platorius Nepos' time, clear traces appear of a radical
change in the planning of the Wall itself. Sections of ditch
already dug are filled up and sections of curtain-wall demolished,
to make room for additional large forts. The original plan had
been the obvious one, to have the Wall as a front line, with local
reserves held back in forts on the Stanegate. Nepos now saw
that it was feasible and desirable to put the counter-attack troops,
the main garrison, in forts on the wall itself, so that counter-
attacks might be mounted instantly. To save the time lost in
sending for troops from the rear, these were now constructed,
some of them with three of their standard four gates opening
north of the connecting curtain wall; and where the ground was
suitable, right, left and right-centre—at Benwell (Condercum),
north of the navigable Tyne, Stanwix (Petriana) north of the Eden
at Carlisle, Chesters and Halton Chesters (Cilurnum and Hunnum)
on either side of the North Tyne—the garrisons were actually
cavalry. Roman soldiers *could*, as Tacitus makes quite clear,
give a good account of themselves in defending walls (*Histories*
ii, 22; iv, 29f); but this was not the plan here. Even the 'mile-
castles' between the main forts were provided with double gates
to the north. Hostile natives who approached would be liable
to be cut off by cavalry, swiftly alerted by visual signalling, as

Professor Birley has suggested, and trapped between them and the great barrier.

That this revision was Nepos' own conception is shown conclusively by a slab of the regular type from Hunnum:

113)   IMP CAES T[RA HADRIANI
                  AVG LEG·VI·V[ICTRIX·P·F
                  A PLATORIO NE[POTE
                  L E G A V G · PR [· PR ·

1427

'The Emperor Caesar Traianus Hadrianus, His Legion VI Victrix Pia Fidelis (built this gate) under Aulus Platorius Nepos, Governor.'

For this is a fort of the revised plan, and the setting up of inscriptions over gates is a sign that the work was finished. It was all done in about four years; though other inscriptions show that a few forts were still to be completed or added under succeeding governors.

The correspondence involved in getting agreement to such radical changes in the plan originally outlined on the spot by Hadrian must have been harassing to the ever-busy emperor; and perhaps it played a part in the process by which his old friend Nepos ultimately—though not finally until after he had returned to Rome—fell from favour.

A Punitive Expedition

So on the frontier there was constant hostility, and columns were no doubt frequently sent forward 'to teach the barbarians a lesson'. We have a record of one such expedition, on a damaged altar from Kirkandrews, close to the Solway. The dedicator's accumulation of names is in the early second century manner, and a reference to 'successes beyond the Wall', in a dedication from the region of Hadrian's work, suggests a period when the Scottish Lowlands were independent.

Later Romans, with their usual irreverence towards the monuments of their predecessors, used this altar as a building-stone and cut down its ornamental top. The beginning of the inscription has thus been destroyed. That which remains reads:

114)
. . . .

L   IVNIVS   VIC
TORINVS FL · · ·
CAELIANVS LEG
AVG LEG VI VIC
PFOBRES TRANS
VALLVM   PRO
SPERE   GESTAS

2034

'(*To* ——, *dedicated by*) *Lucius Junius Victorinus Flavius*(?) *Caelianus, Legate in command of Legion VI Victrix Pia Fidelis, for successes across the Frontier.*'

THE ROMANS IN THE LAKE DISTRICT

Meanwhile Cumberland (cf. No. 89) still had to be garrisoned. Some fragments of a monumental slab, which once adorned the front gate of Hardknott Fort, facing down Eskdale from its pass through the central mountains of the Lake District, identify its Hadrianic garrison. Recognisable parts of the following letters survive:

115)   (*a*)   ES D   (*b*)   PART
                    NE   AIAN
                    O   M

                                  (*d*)   GAVGPRPR
            (*c*)   OH II   LMATAR

(*a*) and (*b*) show part of the top 'rim' of the stone.

PART in the top line with AIAN below identifies the emperor, as follows: LMATAR in the last line, which, unusually, has larger lettering than the line above, is clearly part of 'De LMATAR(um)'; a cohort of Dalmatians; and the slenderness and closeness together of the II after the OH of C]OH(ort) suggested to Mr R. P. Wright that it is part of the number IIII, rather than II; both the 2nd and 4th Dalmatians being known on the army-list. We have most of the title 'Le]G.AVG.PR.PR.', but no clue to the Governor's name. So

IMP·CA] ES·D [IVI·TRAIANI·] PART [HICI
FILDIVI] NE [RVAE . NEP · TR] AIAN [O ·
HADRIAN] O [· AVGVSTO · PONT ·] M [AX ·
L] EGAVGPRPR
C]O H II [II   D E] L M A T A R

JRS, 1965, p. 222

Mr Wright discusses his restoration fully in *Transactions of the Cumberland and Westmorland Arch. Soc.*, 1965.

§4   THE WARS OF ANTONINUS AND THE ANTONINE WALL

But north of the Wall the tribes continued hostile. Roman officers must soon have been murmuring that the only sound strategy was to advance and reoccupy Agricola's conquests; but Hadrian in his fifties, sick, lonely, frequently in pain, and suspicious, being childless, of plots to succeed him, would have been a formidable person to approach with a suggestion implying that his considered British Policy, carried out with so much trouble, had been a failure. But as soon as he was dead (138), his adopted successor, the amiable senator T. Aurelius Antoninus was quickly prevailed upon to agree to a new forward policy. An inscription from Algeria tells us about the governor selected to carry it out:

Q. Lollius Urbicus

116)   *Q.Lollio M.fil. Quir. Urbico cos., leg.Aug. provinc. Germ. Inferioris, fetiali, legato imp. Hadriani in expedition. Iudaica, qua donatus est hasta pura corona aurea, leg. leg.X Geminae, praet. candidat. Caes., trib. pleb. candidat. Caes., leg.procos. Asiae, quaest. urbis, trib. laticlavio leg.XXII Primigeniae, IIII viro viarum curand., Patrono, d.d.p.p.*

D 1065, from Tiddis, a *pagus* (small town or 'civil parish') in the district of Cirta in Numidia.

'To *Quintus Lollius Urbicus, son of Marcus, of the tribe Quirina, Consul, Imperial Governor of the province of Lower Germany, Fetial priest, general on the staff of the Emperor Hadrian in the Jewish campaign, in which he was decorated with the Silver Spear and the Golden Wreath, G.O.C. Leg.X Gemina, Praetor (the Emperor's candidate), Tribune of the People (the Emperor's candidate), deputy to the Governor of Asia, Quaestor of the City, senatorial Tribune in Leg.XXII Primigenia, member of the Board of Four Curators of the Streets, patron (of this village), by decision of the Council the Parish set up (this statue).'*

d.d.p.p. = decreto decurionum pagus posuit. The village or small country town of Tiddis, probably Urbicus' family home—there had been Roman settlers at Cirta since before 120 B.C.—sets up a monument to its most brilliant son and now Patron, or friend at court.

The inscription gives, as usual, posts in order of distinction, so it begins with the Consulship and gives the rest in reverse chronological order. The career differs from normal only in being particularly brilliant. Starting from the bottom we have this biography:

Lollius, perhaps born in Rome (whence his personal name Urbicus?), clearly enjoyed the necessary wealth and connexions to obtain a nomination for the top (senatorial) grade in the emperor's service. We may guess that his father was in the service, and that the consular Lollii were at least some kind of kin. He obtained his 'cadetship', in one of the better posts, as one of the Board of Four who looked after the streets of Rome, and then as 'Broad-Stripe' (potentially senatorial) Tribune in Leg.XXII in Upper Germany. Back in Rome, he was well enough thought of to become City Quaestor, one of the few among the twenty young quaestors entering the Senate in his year, who had some really responsible work; he was (in Professor Birley's phrase) something like a parliamentary private secretary to the emperor. He then went to Asia to gain experience as *legatus*, a judicial *attaché*, to the senior ex-consul who governed that rich Greek province for a year in nominal independence of the emperor. He had Hadrian's official backing (*candidatus Caesaris*) for the elections in the Senate, which could be quite brisk otherwise, to the grades of Tribune of the People (now purely nominal) and Praetor; which would mean that at thirty he was of praetorian rank and qualified to command a legion: X Gemina, on the Danube. He was then taken by Hadrian on his staff in the *expeditio Iudaica* of 132, against the rebellion of Bar-Cochba, and received the decorations of the Silver Spear and Golden Wreath. At his rank, Trajan would have given him two wreaths and two standards; but Hadrian considered that decorations were being given too lavishly. He was certainly not disappointed with Urbicus, who was shortly promoted to the

THE ANTONINE INVASION OF SCOTLAND

(a) Battle-scene

(b) A *legatus Leg. II Augustae* sacrifices the *Suovetaurilia* (pig, sheep and bull) inaugurating the new *limes*

Reproduced by courtesy of Mr R. P. Wright

Plate 3

consulship and a priesthood, as a Fetial, one of the ancient republican *collegia* whose chief duties had then been the carrying of 'flags of truce' and declarations of war. At the time of erection of the inscription he was commanding on the lower Rhine.

The date is probably 138. Hadrian is dead (not called Augustus) but not yet deified, an honour which Antoninus had to press the Senate to vote him; for Hadrian had executed several senators on suspicion of conspiracy, and had not been popular with that body. From Germany, Urbicus was probably transferred direct to Britain in 139.

THE ANTONINE WALL

In swift campaigns, of which we have no narrative, the Romans advanced again to mid-Scotland, and built the great turf bank, guarded by no less than twenty stone-built forts, on the 37-mile line from Old Kilpatrick, north of the tidal Clyde, to Carriden on the Forth. Other forts continued the line along the south coasts of the two firths. Seventeen 'distance-slabs' commemorate the lengths of wall and ditch constructed by each of the three legions. The finest of them, from the end of the wall at Bridgeness on the Forth, has the distinction of being illustrated. Left, a Roman cavalryman charges through and over four naked enemies with short spears and small, oblong (wooden?) shields with round bosses. Right, a Legate (the Governor and Fetial Priest Lollius Urbicus himself?) prepares to offer the great sacrifice of Pig, Sheep and Bull, *suovetaurilia,* inaugurating the new frontier works. He pours a libation from a *patera* over an altar of the shape well represented in our museums. In front, a squatting musician plays on a double pipe, while the victims await their doom; behind, over the heads of the bystanders, a legionary *vexillum*
carries the legend: II . And between the reliefs the main text, typically of all the less elaborately decorated building-slabs, reads:

LEG
AUG

117)   I M P · CAES · TITO · AELIO
          H A D R I · ANTONINO
          AVG · PIO · P · P · LEG II
          AVG   PER   MP IIII DCLII

2139   F E C   [Plate 3]

'*To the Emperor Caesar Titus Aelius Hadrianus Antoninus Augustus the Good: Legion II Augusta built this, for a distance of four miles, 652 paces.*'

(*Per milia passuum IIII,* (*passus*) *DCLII, fecit.*) The emperor, like his predecessor, takes his adoptive father's names. AELIO can be seen to be slightly squeezed on the stone.

FORTS IN REAR

Two roads, well marked by Roman camps and forts, led north from the old frontier—one from Carlisle into Clydesdale, the other from Corbridge, by way of Trimontium, Newstead on the Tweed. On the latter, a long march north of Corbridge, lay a fort destined to a long and useful career, Bremenium, High Rochester, in Redesdale, high up among the Cheviot Hills. A building-inscription names the general and also shows the work of the auxilia in building as well as fighting.

118)

IMP · CAES · T · AELIO
HD·ANTONINO·AVG·PIO·P·P
SVB · Q · LOL · VRBICO
LEG · AVG · PRO · PRAE
COH · I LING

1276   EQ·F

'*For the Emperor Caesar Titus Aelius Hadrianus Antoninus Augustus Pius, Father of his Country; under Quintus Lollius Urbicus, Legatus Augusti Pro Praetore (i.e. Governor of Britain, cf. No. 28), the 1st Lingones (part mounted) built this.*'

—AND IN FRONT

Archaeology has made it quite clear that the Antonine occupation did not stop at the Isthmus, but took in all the good farming land, the relatively populous area, south-east of the Highland Line, as far as Agricola's old fort of Cardean in Strathmore. Inscriptions are very rare north of the Wall; but one, which though brief is complete and datable, has the distinction of being the northern-most of all known inscribed stones of the empire.

Loyal dedications by soldiers to the Virtus (valour) and other high qualities of the emperor are common. Comparatively rare are some to the Emperor's Discipline; they appear under Hadrian, a stern disciplinarian and yet popular with his troops for his attention to them and frequent sharing of their life, and continue under Antoninus. From the bed of the River Almond near the Roman fort called Bertha, not far from Perth, comes a slab (not an altar) perhaps meant for the wall of the fort's Chapel of the Standards, with the text:

119)   DISCIPVL

                               INAE

                               AVGVSTI

JRS XLIX (1959), p. 136

'To the Discipline of His Majesty.'

Meanwhile Hadrian's Wall was evacuated; even its gates were taken off, probably for re-use elsewhere, and the arches left standing open. This, however, proved over-optimistic.

Active operations were over in the year 146, at which date, as the Chesters Diploma shows, Lollius Urbicus had been recalled and the Emperor was granting dismissal to time-expired soldiers. An issue of coins, a great number of which found their way to this frontier, was struck to commemorate the campaign. They bear the image and superscription of BRITANNIA, and the date, the Emperor's fourth consulship, A.D. 145.

THE REBELLION OF 155-7

Once more peace lasted for less than twenty years. Once more, as when under Agricola the troops had been strung out from the Trent to the Clyde, the turbulent Brigantes seemed to see their opportunity, and the inscriptions tell again of troops sent from Germany to supplement the depleted legions, and of ruined forts that had to be rebuilt, from the Scottish Lowlands to Derbyshire.

120)   IMP · ANTONI

                               NO · AVG · PIO · P

                               PAT ·   VEXILATIO

                               LEG·II·AVG·ET·LEG

                               · VI · VIC · ET · LEG ·

                               · XX · VV · CONR

                               BVTI · EX · GER · DV

                               OBVS·SVB·IVLIO·VE

1322   RO·LEG·AVG·PR·P·

'To the Emperor Antoninus Augustus Pius, Father of his Country, the Draft for Legions II Augusta, VI Victrix, and XX Valeria Victrix, contributed from the two German Provinces, under Julius Verus, Governor of Britain, (set up this slab).'

This inscription, like Nos. 96-97, was dredged out of the Tyne at Newcastle 'in the North Channel of the Swing Bridge. The neatness of the work and the absolute lack of weathering of the stone was remarkable; as is the omission of one L in *vexil(l)atio* and the T and first I in *con(t)r(i)buti*' (Collingwood).

Two slabs, smashed but admitting of confident restoration, commemorate the rebuilding of cohort-posts, from the extreme south and north respectively of the Brigantian country.

121)   I M P · CAESARI · T · [AEL · HADR ·
                 AN]TONINO · AV[G · PIO · P · P ·
                 COH   ·   I   ·   AQVITA[NORVM
                 SVB · IVLIO · VER[O · LEG ·] AVG
                 PR·PR·INSTA[NTE]   (vacant space)
                 C]APITON[IO   ·   FV]SCO   PRAE

283

From Brough-on-Noe, Derbyshire—Navio, the fort that dominated the lead-mining country.

'For the Emperor Caesar Titus Aelius Hadrianus Antoninus Augustus Pius, Father of his Country, under Julius Verus, Governor of Britain, the 1st Aquitanian Cohort, commanded by Capitonius Fuscus (erected these buildings).'

The fort is only two acres in area, so that half the unit at any one time must have been stationed elsewhere.

122)   I M P · CAES · T · A[EL H]ADR ·
                 AN[TO]NINO · AVG · [PIO · PO]NT ·
                 MAX·[TRIB·] POT·XXI·COS IIII·
                 COH·II [TVNG]R· MIL·EQ·C·L·
                 SVB·IV[L·VERO·] LEG·AVG·PR·PR

From Birrens, in Dumfries, Blatobulgium, garrisoned, as many less battered inscriptions confirm, by the 2nd Tungrians, a *cohors milliaria equitata* of horse and foot 960 strong, the most formidable type of auxiliary cohort. Its men had at some unknown date been honoured with the privileges of the partial citizenship known by the old republican term of 'Latin rights', and the regiment continued to mention this distinction even after the edict of 211 had extended full Roman citizenship to all provincials.

'For the Emperor Caesar Titus Aelius Hadrianus Antoninus Augustus Pius, Pontifex Maximus, in the twenty-first year of his reign, four times Consul, the Second Tungrian part-mounted Cohort, 1000 strong, Latin Citizens, under Julius Verus, Governor of Britain, (erected these buildings).

The year—A.D. 158—enables us to date the final suppression of the rebellion.

§5 THE ROMAN OCCUPATION IN SCOTLAND

A few score of inscriptions, then, remain to tell us of the not unbroken peace of those fifty years, about 140-90, during which for the second time the Romans occupied southern Scotland. Some, as we have seen, tell of wars and rebellions, building and rebuilding, the names and dates of governors. Others give a glimpse here and there of the individuals who dwelt in those carefully sited and fortified cohort-posts along the line of the frontier and the great trunk-roads. Epitaphs sometimes do this for us; but the inscriptions that do it best are the religious dedications. It is these that tell us of the fidelity of some Belgian soldiers, when they had worshipped Jupiter and the Emperor officially, to a deity of their homeland, or of the anxiety of a freedman for the safety of an officer, his master, or of the hungry religious instincts of the centurion who worshipped many gods at Auchendavy on the Antonine Wall.

First, a group from Birrens:

'CHURCH PARADE'

123)

```
I   ·   O   ·   M
COH      ·      I
N E R V A N A
G E R M A N O R
∞  ·  EQ  ·  CVI
PRAEEST·L·FAENI
VS · FELIX · TRIB
```

'*To Jupiter, Best and Greatest, the 1st German, Emperor Nerva's Own, mixed Battalion, 1000 strong, commanded by Lucius Faenius Felix, Tribune, (dedicate this altar).*'

This regiment was probably at Birrens before the rebellion of 155; the Tungrians replace them afterwards.

124)

D I S C I P ·

AVG·

COH · II ·

T V N G R ·

MIL·EQ·C·L·

2092

'*To the Discipline of His Majesty, the 2nd Tungrians, Part-mounted, 1000 strong, Latin Citizens, (dedicate this altar).*'

PRIVATE PRAYERS

125)

DEAE   VIRADEC

THI PAGVS CON

DRVSTIS   MILIT

IN COH II TVN

GROR SVB SILVI

O AVSPICE PRAEF

2108

'*To the Goddess Viradecthis, men of the Condrustian canton serving in the 2nd Tungrian Cohort, under Silvius Auspex, Commandant.*'

The Pagus Condrustis is a tract of rough country near Liège (still known as Condrost). This Belgian regiment still receives recruits from its original home.

The Goddess Viradecthis (with sundry small variations of spelling) reappears in two or three dedications from the continent.

THE NERVII AT ROUGH CASTLE

'That day he overcame the Nervii' was also a day when that gallant people nearly brought the career of Julius Caesar to a premature end. (*Gallic War*, Book ii, must have been on Shakespeare's school reading list.) The memory adds piquancy to the long service of Nervian cohorts in the Roman army, not least in

Britain (cf. No. 100). Two stones from Rough Castle, west of Falkirk, commemorate their work.

This fort with its defended annexe—wagon and animal park, it is now thought, rather than quarters for families—and the bank and ditch east of it are, by the way, the best-preserved part of the Antonine *limes*. Within easy walking distance of Bonny-bridge on road A808, they well repay a visit. The fort is so small —little over an acre—that it can never have housed more than half a cohort of 480 men. It would appear that, while its head-quarters were here, most of the unit must regularly have been out on patrolling duties (cf. No. 121).

A BUILDING SLAB	AN ALTAR
126) IMP·CA]ESARI·TITO	127) VICTORIAE
AELIO·] HADRIANO·	COH VI NER
ANTO]NINO·AVG·	VIORVM·C·C·
PIO·] P·P·COH · VI ·	FL·BETTO⟩LEG
· NER]VIORVM · PRI ·	XX VV ·
NCI]PIA · FECIT	V · S · L · L · M ·
2145	2144

'For the Emperor T. Aelius An-toninus Pius, pater patriae, the 6th Nervian Cohort built these Head-quarters.'

'To Victory, the 6th Nervian Cohort under acting command of Flavius Betto, Centurion in Leg. XX Valeria Victrix, gladly, willingly and duly paid its vow.'

C.C. = *cuius curam* (*agit*), = 'i/c.' as distinct from 'o.c.'

V.S.L.L.M. = *votum solvit laeta libens merito*, the regular formula on offerings made in payment for services prayed for, such as victory.

SYRIAN ARCHERS

Most of the light infantry were Belgians and Rhinelanders; but one solitary oriental regiment was brought all the way to Britain and long remained, recruited from its original home land: sharpshooters from the ancient Hamath, modern Hamah. The government knew, someone has said, that the best archers were born in Syria and could not be made elsewhere. They first appear in Pompeius Falco's army in the great Diploma, No. 100.

And at least sometimes, the sensible course was taken of sending officers who knew the east to command them, as when they garrisoned the Bar Hill fort near Kirkintilloch, probably after 158:

128)   d]EO · SILV[ANO

                              c]ARISTAN[IVS

                              I]VSTIANV[S

                              PRAEF

                              c]OH I HAM[IOR

                              V·S·L·L·M

2167

'*To the god Silvanus, Caristanius Justianus, Officer Commanding the 1st Hamian Archers, gladly, willingly and duly pays his vow.*'

Caristanius bears the same rare family name as Agricola's sometime G.O.C. IX Legion; but he is hardly his descendant, or he would be of senatorial rank, and the command of an auxiliary battalion would be beneath him. He is probably therefore of the branch of the family still equestrian and still domiciled at Pisidian Antioch.

A Brigantian Soldier

A tombstone also shows something unique to us, and *perhaps* rare in its time: a Brigantian tribesman serving in the Antonine army in Britain. British conscripts, as we have seen, were usually packed off overseas. Perhaps this man volunteered for service. Even so, his name and his father's show an interesting development. Two generations before this stone was set up, so about Agricola's time, a Brigantian of the Romanising party had given his son the Latin name Vindex; but Vindex gave *his* son a British name. That son, nevertheless, was accepted for service in the Roman army *in Britain*—probably before rather than after the great rebellion of 155-7. But the names illustrate the tension that must have been set up in thousands of Brigantian families and individuals, between civilisation and freedom.

It is a roughly cut stone, from Mumrills near Falkirk, now at Edinburgh. The letters, which still bear traces of red paint, *in*crease in size from top to bottom, a rarity.

129)

DIS·M·NECTOVELIVS·F
· VINDICIS · AN · IXXX
STIP · VIIII · NAT
IONIS · BRIGANS
MILITAVIT · IN
COH · II · THR

2142

'To the Spirits of the Departed. Nectovelius, son of Vindex, aged 29, nine years a soldier, a Brigantian, served in the 2nd Thracian Cohort.'

An Ex-Slave and his Master

130)

FORTVNAE   P[RO
SALVTE P CAMPA[NI
ITALICI PRAEF COH [II
TVN CELER LIBERTVS
[V]S L L M

2094

'To Fortune, for the safety of Publius Campanius Italicus, Officer Commanding the 2nd Tungrian Cohort, Celer his freedman gladly, willingly and duly pays his vow.'

From Birrens.

The inscription accompanied the offering of an image of the goddess 'Good Luck', in relief—perhaps vowed by Celer when Italicus was absent on a campaign.

At Trimontium on the Tweed, 'the strategic centre of the Lowlands', as Collingwood called it, the great fort of Newstead, no less than four times reconstructed, was an advanced base, more than an ordinary cohort-post. Here we meet with legionaries, including legionary centurions, who make dedications to gods of the classical pantheon:

131)

I · O · M
G · ARRIVS
DOMITIANVS
⟩ LEG · XX · V · V
V · S · L · L · M

2123

'To Jupiter Best and Greatest, Gaius Arrius Domitianus, Centurion in Legion XX Valeria Victrix pays his vow, gladly, willingly and duly.'

132)   D E O
                        A P O L L I N I
                    L · MAXIMIVS
                    GAETVLICVS · ⟩
                          LEG
2120

'*To Apollo; (dedicated by) Lucius Maximus Gaetulicus, Legionary Centurion*'.

For Maximius Gaetulicus, cf. No. 159. There, he is in Leg. XX; omission of a number here is curious, but he may have been in the middle of a transfer.

The dedication of the archer-god is appropriately decorated; to the left is sculptured a quiver full of arrows, to the right a bow.

Among relics of ordinary daily life from Roman Scotland appear a fine series of old boots and shoes, including some for women and children, from various fort ditches; the usual Samian pottery, often stamped with known and datable makers' names; and from Newstead, a bronze bowl, carefully marked in punched letters with the name of the mess it belonged to:

133)   TVRM CRISPI
                                 NIGRI

RIB II

'*Crispus Niger's Troop*'

Another example of the short inscriptions on things of daily use is on a silver ring found near East Kilbride:

134)   VTERE FELIX
RIB II

'*Good luck to the user.*'

CIVILIANS IN ROMAN SCOTLAND

A Lothian farmer, ploughing deep in the modern manner in 1956 at Carriden on the Firth of Forth, where stood the eastern-most fort of the wall, made a discovery of importance:

135)

I   O   M

VICANI   CONSI[S

TENTES   CASTEL[LO

VELVNIATE   CV[RAM

AGENTE   AEL·MAN

SVETO   V S L L M

JRS XLVI, 1957

'To Jupiter Optimus Maximus, the settlers of the village at the Fort of Veluniate pay their vow gladly, willingly and duly. Aelius Mansuetus superintended the work.'

First, this stone gives us our first fixed name for a fort on the Antonine Wall. The late Ravenna List of place-names of Roman Britain gives indeed ten names of such forts, beginning with Velunia (sic), but since there are twenty in all, more than ten being of considerable size, any assignment of the other nine still remains speculative. However, this discovery leaves us not without hope for more. Second, it is our first explicit evidence of settlers, presumably traders, 'established' (the word consistentes appears, similarly used, on the Rhine), and with their own recognised local government at the lowest level, that of a vicus, used both of a village and a town 'quarter'. What did they trade in? 'Trade goods' against slaves, no doubt; salt, probably (see below, p. 107); furs, perhaps; gold if they could get it; but the amount of gold to be had in Britain was on the whole a disappointment to the Romans.

The existence of this settlement however justifies recognising as belonging to civilian rather than to army families a few tomb-stones of women and children, on which no regiment is mentioned. One, from Auchendavy in the central sector, is of particular interest:

136)

D·M·

SALMANES

VIX·AN·XV

SALMANES

POSUIT

2182

'(Dis Manibus). Salmanes lived fifteen years. Salmanes set this up.'

The name of the deceased and (presumably) his father is
Semitic; in fact, Solomon; perhaps a Syrian trader.

The Centurion of Auchendavy

But the individual best known to us in Roman Scotland is still,
beyond a doubt, the centurion who when stationed at Auchendavy
dedicated to various deities no less than four of the little altars
that were the customary form of durable offering. One is to
Jupiter Optimus Maximus; one to Diana and Apollo *in this order*,
probably the Great Goddess and Young God of Thrace, a hint
of the dedicator's origins. The other two follow:

137)

M A R T I
MINERVAE
CAMPESTRI
BVS   HERCL
EPONAE
VICTORIAE
M · COCCEI
F I R M V S

2177   ⟩ LEG II AVG

*'To Mars and Minerva, Guardians of the Parade-Ground (?), to
Hercules, to Epona, and to Victory; dedicated by Marcus Cocceius
Firmus, Centurion in Legion II Augusta.'*

The dedication is to the various war-gods; Minerva is here
identified with the warlike Greek Athene. *Campestres* is either an
epithet both of Mars and of Minerva, or, possibly = 'The Spirits
of the Parade-Ground'. Epona is a Gallic goddess of the Horse.
Gaul seems to have given Italy the thoroughbred horse; Strabo
the geographer (under Augustus) describes the Gallic regiments
as the best cavalry in the Roman army, and Arrian comments on
the number of Celtic words in the cavalry drill-book. Even the
spoken Latin of educated Romans contained several 'horsey'
words that hailed from Gaul, such as *mannus*, a pony, and *petorritum*,
'four-wheeler', a carriage. The Latin *equus* is to *Epo* as *quattuor* to
Gallic *petor*, four—modern Cumbrian *pethera*, which figures
among the Celtic numerals used on the fells within this century
for counting a score of sheep.

138)   G E N I O   ·
                  T E R R A E
                  B R I T A
                  N N I C A E
                  M C O C C E I
                  F I R M V S
2175   ⟩ LEG II AVG

'*To the Spirit of the Land of Britain; Marcus Cocceius Firmus, Centurion in Legion II Augusta, (dedicates this).*'

As it happens, we probably know something of this same Cocceius Firmus from another source. A jurist who flourished under Marcus Aurelius, quoted in Justinian's *Digest* (xlix, 15), cites a case illustrating Treasury liability:

'*A woman who had been condemned for a crime to hard labour in the salt-works*' (where, as we read in another passage, female convicts cooked and washed for the male) '*was captured by raiders from across the border, sold in the normal way of trade, and so returned to her original condition. The Treasury had to pay the price of her repurchase to the centurion Cocceius Firmus.*'

The name Cocceius is a rare one, probably implying citizenship obtained by an ancestor from the emperor Cocceius Nerva, who only reigned for two years; and as Professor Birley has argued,[1] the conditions, with salt-works (on the Forth?) adjacent to a disturbed frontier, suit Roman Scotland very well. We naturally feel sympathy chiefly for the woman, evidently a slave of Firmus before she was a convict. What treatment was it that led her into desperate courses? But if the religious centurion was also 'an hard man' in private life, he was not the last example of such a syndrome in the history of Scotland.

THE ROMAN ARMY UNDER STRAIN

After 158, every effort was made to strengthen Rome's grip on the north. Hadrian's Wall was reoccupied and for a time *both* walls were held. But this produced new problems. There simply were not enough auxiliary cohorts. Small forts were built, hold-

[1] In *Roman Britain and the Roman Army*, pp. 88ff. (with more about Firmus' possible origins and career).

ing part of a cohort, as at Brough-on-Noe and Rough Castle (Nos. 121, 126-7). Even so, it is calculated that all the forts believed to have been held at this time would have required over 50,000 men; evidence of a considerable potentially hostile population. Recourse was had to legionary detachments, as at Newstead and (probably now, though the inscriptions are undated) at House-steads on Hadrian's Wall:

139)	I · O · M	140)	COCIDIO E[T
	ET DEO COCIDIO		GENIO · PR[AE
	GENIOQ · HVIS		SIDI · VALE
	LOCI · MIL · LEG		RIVS · M · L[E
	II·AVG AGENTES		G·VI·V·P·F·VP
	IN · PRAESIDIO		
	V S L M		
1583		1577	

'To Jupiter Best and Greatest, and to the God Cocidius, and to the Spirit of this place, Soldiers of Legion II Augusta serving as garrison willingly and duly paid their vow.'

'To Cocidius and the Luck of the Fort, Valerius, Soldier in Legion VI Victrix Pia Fidelis, set this up in payment of his vow.'

VP = votum posuit.

Q = que and HVIS, huius.

Cocidius, whose name means 'the Red One', was a local war-god, whom the Romans identify with Mars (cf. No. 154). No doubt the face of his idol at Fanum Cocidi, a place-name in the Ravenna List somewhere in south-west Northumberland, was painted red.

But this dissipation of legionary strength in detachments, a measure of sheer necessity, was in direct contravention of the military principle that reserves and shock troops must not be committed to the defence of outposts. The fact was that the Roman army in Britain was overstretched. The situation was ominous.

THE END OF ROMAN SCOTLAND

Another twenty years passed, and again, a new generation of young warriors having grown up, the northern tribes were ready to try conclusions with Rome. And the result this time put back the frontier permanently to the Cheviot Hills. Dio Cassius mentions a rebellion in the reign of Marcus Aurelius, and another early in that of Commodus, his unworthy son (soon after 180) in which a Roman *legatus* was defeated and killed. Order was restored by Ulpius Marcellus (cf. Nos. 167, 187) a former governor of Britain sent back to his old province to deal with the crisis, and inscriptions at Rome show that Commodus took the title of Britannicus, Conqueror of Britain, about 184. One might suppose that a victory had been won. No doubt it had, but archaeology shows clearly that Marcellus, like Hadrian before him, decided that the great tract of country stretching up to the Antonine Wall could not be held without an increase in the strength of the British army which the province, already a liability, not a financial asset to the Empire,[1] could not afford.

Certain information of the loss of the Scottish Lowlands at this date is given especially by those smallest and commonest of written documents, coins—by their absence. From the age of the Antonines many of these are known from the Roman forts in Scotland; from later generations, none. Even Birrens, one day's march from Carlisle, was abandoned; the 2nd Tungrians appear henceforth at Castlesteads, on Hadrian's Wall.

In an inscription from Carlisle, unfortunately a fragment, a Roman officer speaks of the valiant resistance of his fellow-soldiers against the barbarian attacks. The surviving portion is as follows:

141)

DEI	·	HERC	....
VICTI	·	CON	....
TIBVS	· PRO ·	S	....
C O M M	I L I T O	N	....
B A R B	A R O	R	....
O B V	I R T	V	....
P	·	SEXTANI	.
TAT	·	TRAIA	

946

The inscription is on a slab of red sandstone, forming the top of a small arch. As Haverfield pointed out, the fact that more than

[1] Appian, *Proem*, 5.

half of the arch is missing shows that we have also lost more than half the words. Under the circumstances it is impossible to restore with certainty anything that is not a mere list of an emperor's titles; but Haverfield suggested something like the following as giving at any rate the sense which the surviving words demand.

The mention of Hercules dates the slab to the reign of Commodus, who loved to be adored by his flatterers as 'the Roman Hercules'.

```
         DEI · HERCVLIS · AVGVSTI · IN
         VICTI · CONSERVATORIS · COMI
         TIBVS·PRO·SALVTE·DOMINI·N·ET
         COMMILITONVM · FVSA · INGENTI
         BARBARORVM  ·  MVLTITVDINE
         OBVIRTVTEM      ·      DEDICAVIT
         P · SEXTANIVS · ——— · EX · CIVI
         TAT · TRAIA          NENSIVM
```

'*To the Comrades of the God Hercules the Invincible, the Saviour, for the welfare of our Prince and of his fellow soldiers, who put to flight a great host of Barbarians; for their valour, Publius Sextanius ——, Prefect, of the City of Trajan, dedicated this.*'

See Wright's notes to *RIB* 946 for other possible readings and discussion.

The 'City of Trajan' here is probably the Colonia Ulpia Traianensis, formerly Castra Vetera, Xanten on the lower Rhine.

CHAPTER IV

LIFE ON HADRIAN'S WALL

After this for nearly two centuries, the great wall between Tyne and Solway remained the backbone of the frontier system. A good half of all the Roman inscriptions in Britain come from the wall and its supporting stations.

Perhaps the best introduction to these original documents of the Roman frontier is to look at a selection of those from one typical station.

§1   VERCOVICIUM

Vercovicium, Housesteads, lies about thirty miles from New-castle, where the central section of the wall looks out across the high moors from the cliffs of the Great Whin Sill. Here the First Tungrian Cohort lay in garrison for over a hundred and fifty years, from the second century to the fourth.

The regiment in its corporate capacity naturally conforms to the State religion, as several altars witness.

142)   I   O   M
                        ET   NVMINIBVS
                        AVG · COH · I · TV
                        N G R O R V M
                        MIL · CVI · PRAEE
                        ST · Q · VERIVS ·
                        S U P E R S T I S
1586   P R A E F E C T V S

'*To Jupiter Best and Greatest, and to the Deities of the Emperors; (dedicated by) the First Tungrian Cohort, 1000 strong, under the command of Quintus Verius Superstes, Prefect.*'

143)   HERCVLI
                        COH · I · TVNGROR
                        MIL·
                        CVI·PRAEEST·P·AEL
1580   MODESTVS · PRAEF ·

'To Hercules; (dedicated by) the First Tungrian Cohort, 1000 strong, under the command of Publius Aelius Modestus, Prefect.'

The choice of Hercules as a deity for official worship probably dates the inscription to the reign of Commodus (cf. No. 141).

So also the commanding officers—Roman 'knights', usually from Gaul, Spain or Italy, dedicate to the gods of the classical pantheon, even individually:

144)

```
          D     E     O
        MARTI   QVIN
        FLORIVS   MA
        TERNVS PRAEF
        COH · I · TVNG
          V·S·L·M
```

1591

'To the God Mars, Quintus Florius Maternus, officer commanding the First Tungrian Cohort, willingly and duly pays his vow.'

But the Celtic or German soldier, left to himself, here as elsewhere worships humbler deities, of whom classical literature has nothing to say:

145)

```
          D E O
        _____

        H V I T R I
        A S P V A N I S
        PRO   ET   SVIS
        _____

          V O T
          S O L
```

1603

'To the God Huiter, Aspuanis pays his vow, for (himself) and his.'

The word SE seems to have been left out, after PRO.

The god Huiter (whose name is given in different inscriptions in a fine variety of spellings, and more often in the plural, *di Vitires* and the like) seems to have been a native German god or group of gods from the Rhineland. He, or they, became popular on the British frontier, and a spelling often found is *di Veteres*, as though it were a Latin title, 'To the Old Gods'.

Germanic war-gods are particularly well represented at Housesteads, where the Tungrian Cohort long continued to be recruited from the Low Countries, and where later are found new units of tribesmen, supplementing the Cohort and perhaps under its command. One six-foot-tall, square inscribed pillar has been recognised as the left doorpost of a shrine, where German soldiers worshipped their own 'Mars' and the Alaisiagae, perhaps Valkyries:

146)
<pre>
              D E O
            M A R T I ·
        T H I N C S O
        ET   DVABVS   ·
        A L A I S I A G I S ·
        BEDE · ET · FI
        MMILENE   ·
        ET · N · AVG · GER
        M · CIVES · TV
        I H A N T I
1593   V S LM
</pre>

'*To the God Mars Thincsus and the two Alaisiagae Beda and Fimmilena, and to the deity of the Emperor, German tribesmen of Tuihantis willingly and duly pay their vow.*'

The title Thincsus has been associated with Norse 'Thing', and if so would mean 'of the place of council'; and Tuihantis may be the district still called Twenthe, in the Over-Yssel province of Holland.

N.AVG. = *numen Augusti.*

147)
<pre>
         D   E   O
        MARTI · ET · DVABVS
        ALAISIAGIS·ET·N·AVG
        GER·CIVES·TVIHANTI
        CVNEI · FRISIORVM
        VER · SER · ALEXAN
        DRIANI · V O T V M
        S O L V E R V N T
        L I B E N T [E S
1594   M
</pre>

148)
<pre>
        D E A B V S
        A L A I S I A
        G I S · B A V
        DIHILLIE
        ET · FRIAGA
        BI·ET·N·AVG
        N · H N A V
        D I F R I D I
        V   S L M
</pre>

(147) *'To the God Mars and the two Alaisiagae and the Deity of the Emperor, the German tribesmen of Tuihantis of the Assault Battalion of Frisians of Vercovicium, Severus Alexander's Own, pay their vow willingly and duly.'*

CVNEVS, translated 'Assault-Battalion', = literally 'wedge', a standard German formation. The phrase SER (for SEVER.?) ALEXANDRIANI dates the stone to Severus Alexander's reign; he was murdered in 235; and the abbreviation VER is currently explained as for 'Vercovician', and considered to give the proper form of the name of the fort. The much later official address-list called the *Notitia Dignitatum* (which names the 1st Tungrian Cohort as still in occupation, perhaps anachronistically), gives the name as Borcovicium, as found in earlier modern books. For B replacing V in late Latin, cf. No. 79; while -OR- could interchange with -ER- (cf. Kerkyra, Corcyra) where the R was strongly rolled. Regiments in the third century begin frequently to be named after their permanent stations.

(148) *'To the goddesses the Alaisiagae Baudihillia and Friagabis and to the Deity of the Emperor, Hnaudifridus' Company willingly and duly pays its vow.'*

'Hnaudifridus' has been recognised as the German name Notfried. The N before the name stands for *Numerus*, 'irregular unit'. What is interesting here is the appearance (in the third century?) of such a unit under a German chief as its commander, a phenomenon increasingly common in the late empire.

It is noticeable that these tribal Germans always associate the *Numen* of the Emperor in the worship of their own war-gods; and there is no need to suppose that this was merely conventional. Personal loyalty to his commander is mentioned in Tacitus' *Germania* as a characteristic of the German warrior, and it was one of the qualities which made German soldiers so useful to Rome.

Outside the fort, as the generations passed, a village grew up, in which lived the wives and children of the soldiers, with a floating population of traders, shopkeepers, and other hangers-on. One such will have been the priest Apollonius, with his Greek name, who makes a dedication to the Greek personification of Jealous Fate:

149)   D E A E
                              _____

                         N E M E S I
                         A P O L L O N
                         IVS   SACE
2065   RDOS   FEC

'*To the Goddess Nemesis, Apollonius the Priest made this.*'

And like many a Roman frontier station, Vercovicium had its
Mithraeum—an underground cave of the usual type, cut into the
rock among the houses and garden-plots on the terraced hillside
south of the fort, where the faithful—officers, under-officers and
the better-educated legionaries, mostly, rather than the rougher
auxiliaries—might be washed in the blood of the victim, initiated
into the successive grades of the 'freemasonry', and take comfort
from its assurance that they were working with God to establish
and defend peace, law, and righteousness throughout the world.
The following is one of several dedications to him from Housesteads:

150)   D   E   O
                        SOLI   ·   INVI
                        CTO   MYTRAE
                        S A E C V L A R I
                        L I T O R I V S
                        P A C A T I A N V S
                        BF · COS · PRO
                        SE ET SVIS · V · S
1599   L·M·

'*To the God, the Sun, Invincible, Mithras the Eternal, Litorius Pacatianus
beneficiary of the Consular (Governor), pays his vow willingly and duly, for
himself and his.*'

'Consular beneficiary': a soldier seconded for special work by
the Governor-General of the province (cf. Nos. 17, 91).

§2   RELIGIOUS INSCRIPTIONS
            FROM OTHER STATIONS

In 1949 another Mithraeum was discovered, at the next fort east of
Housesteads, Carrawburgh (Brocolitia), with a group of three

R.B.—I

altars dedicated by commanders of the garrison, all probably in
the early third century. That on the left (west) gives the god's
name in full, and shows him in relief, rising out of the rock, with
radiate halo. That in the centre can be roughly dated. That on
the right has a special interest of its own:

151)	(sculpture)	152)	DEO · INV · M	153)	D · IN · M · S ·
			L · ANTONIVS		AVL · CLVENTIVS
	DEO · INVICTO ·		P R O C V LVS		HABITVS · PRAEF
	MITRAE · M · SIM		PRAEF·COH·I·BAT		· C O H · I
	PLICIVS·SIMPLEX		ANTONINIANAE		B A T A V O R V M
	PREF · V · S · L · M		· V · S · L · M ·		D O M V V L T I
1546		1544			N A · C O L O N ·
					S E P T · A V R · L
					V · S · L · M ·

1545

(151) 'To *the Invincible God Mithras, Marcus Simplicius Simplex,
Commandant, willingly and duly pays his vow.*'

PREF for PRAEF(ectus) shows the E for classical Æ, which is
standard in the Middle Ages, beginning to creep in.

(152) 'To *the Invincible God Mithras, Lucius Antonius Proculus,
commanding the 1st Batavian Cohort, Antoninus' Own, willingly and duly
pays his vow.*'

The Regiment's title, ANTONINIANA, roughly dates the altar; for
it is characteristic *not* of the reigns of Titus and Marcus Antoninus,
but of the dynasty of Severus, who, as we shall see in the next
chapter, was at pains to affiliate his family to the revered Antonine
house. The title is characteristic of the reigns of Caracalla and
Elagabalus, by the end of which (A.D. 222) it had become some-
what tarnished, and fell out of use.

(153) '*Sacred to the Invincible God Mithras. Aulus Cluentius Habitus,
commanding the 1st Batavian Cohort, of the tribe Voltinia, from Colonia
Septimia Aurelia, Larinum, willingly and duly pays his vow.*'

The first line abbreviates *Deo Invicto Mithrae Sacrum.*

This dedicator gives his Roman tribe, in a manner long disused
in most inscriptions, and even the first three letters of his *praenomen,*
which even under the Republic was customarily reduced to an
initial. Why? The reason is pride of family; for this family,

though never senatorial, had been famous to readers of the classics for nearly 300 years, ever since Cicero defended another Aulus Cluentius Habitus, and obtained his acquittal on a charge of murder of which he was probably guilty, in a famous trial with political overtones. The Cluentii were a great family of south Italy, where Severus had now elevated their native town of Larinum to the rank of a Roman Colony. Vergil in the *Aeneid* had asserted their descent from the Trojans. And here they are, represented in Britain in the early third century, still plain equestrian gentlemen—but still there.

154)

> MARTI COC M
> LEG II AVG
> Ɔ SANCTIANA
> Ɔ SECVNDINI
> D·SOL·SVB CV
> RA·AELIANI C
> CVRA·OPPIVS
> F]ELIX·OPTIO

2024

'*To Mars Cocidius Soldiers of Legion II Augusta, Companies of Sanctius and Secundinus, pay their vow, under the superintendence of Aelianus, Centurion; Oppius Felix, Under-Officer, took charge of the work.*'

For Mars Cocidius, cf. Nos. 141, 143.

SANCTIANA (not -I) seems to follow a practice used in giving the late centurion's name when the post was vacant.

D·SOL probably = *Donum solvunt*. CVRA = *curavit*.

From the Wall near Stanwix, Carlisle. A dedication by two centuries jointly, each appointing its representative, is a rarity; perhaps the vow was made when the two companies were together in some tight corner.

Another local deity was worshipped chiefly in Cumberland; like Cocidius, he was sometimes identified with Mars—Mars Belatucadrus—and like Huiter or Veter, he enjoyed a large variety of spellings. One dedication to him comes from Brocolitia, which, by the way, means Brocksbourne or Badgerhole:

155)   D E O

BELLETI

CAVRO

LVNARIS

1521

'*To the God Belleticaurus, Lunaris (dedicates this).*'

Another, from Brocavum (Brougham, in Westmorland):

156)   D E O

BLATVCAIRO

A V D A G V S

V   S   P   S   S

774

'*To the God Blatucairus, Audagus pays his vow, for himself and his.*'

V S P S S = *votum solvit pro se et suis.*

One small and battered altar a little south of the Wall, from Chester-le-Street, is remarkable for making the Veteres not only plural but feminine:

157)   D A E A B [V

S   V I T I R

I B V S

————————

V I T A L I S

[V   S   L]   M

1047

'*To the Goddesses Vitires, Vitalis willingly and duly pays his vow.*'

DAEABVS is would-be 'correct' for *deabus.*

Among these obscure gods and goddesses one more demands notice—Covventina, a water-nymph, over whose spring near Brocolitia a small temple was built as early as Hadrian's time. It must have been thought lucky to visit the shrine and throw a coin into the cistern—perhaps it was oracular, or a wishing-well— for when the place was discovered by accident in modern times there were found upwards of sixteen thousand small coins, of all ages down to the reign of Gratian (A.D. 380). A sculptured slab shows the nymph in relief—an attractively primitive rendering of the idea of a water-sprite—with the inscription:

158)

D E A E

COVVENTINAE

TD COSCONIA

NVS · PR · COH

I · BAT · L · M

1534

'To the Goddess Covventina, Titus Domitius Cosconianus, Prefect of the 1st Batavian Cohort, willingly and duly dedicates this.'

One bronze coin of Antoninus Pius was particularly common here; several hundred specimens were found. It bears on the reverse the figure of Britannia, disarmed and dejected, with the legend COS IIII - BRITANNIA. The Emperor's fourth consulship was in A.D. 145. The coin evidently commemorates the victories of Lollius Urbicus.

Among the eastern cults, less purely formal than those of classical Rome and more imposing than those of Cocidius or Huiter, one, which gained a popularity second only to Mithraism, was that of Jupiter Dolichenus. He was a storm-god and war-god, related probably to Teshub of the ancient Hittites; an impressive figure, as seen in some sculptures from the Danube frontier, standing on a bull and brandishing a double axe. Roman soldiers discovered him at Dülük on the Euphrates, which the Greeks called Doliche, as it were 'Long-town'; and his altars spread, not in the interior of the Empire, but along the military roads, that followed the Rhine and Danube to the shores of the northern sea. One from Aesica, Great Chesters, west of Housesteads, reads:

159)

I · O · M

DOLICENO LV

CIVS MAXIM

IVS GAETVLIC

VS Ɔ LEG XX VV

V S L M

1725

To Jupiter the Good and Great, of Doliche, Lucius Maximius Gaetulicus, Centurion in Legion XX Valeria Victrix, willingly and duly pays his vow.'

The centurion is the same as the dedicator of No. 132, from Trimontium.

Common, too, in the western provinces are dedications to the Mother-Goddesses. Celtic nature-spirits they seem to have been, connected with the fruits of the earth. A pleasing sculpture from Cirencester represents them, in high relief, holding baskets of fruit and corn. On the Wall they appear repeatedly, as on an altar from Newcastle—'Hadrian's Bridge', Pons Aelii—bearing the home-sick dedication:

160)   DE   MATRIBVS   TRAMARINIS [B V
               A   PATRIS AVRELIVS IVVENALIS [S
1318

PATRIS is presumably for *patriis.*
'*Aurelius Juvenalis (dedicates this) to the Mother-Goddesses of his own land over the sea.*'

SPORT AND THE COUNTRYSIDE

Yet other dedications tell us something of the Roman soldier's sparetime occupations. Of these the favourite, as we should expect, was hunting, which was also not unimportant as a source of meat. From some way south of the wall, in county Durham, comes this:

161)   SILVANO   INVICTO   SAC
               C TETIVS·VETVRIVS·MICIA
               NVS·PRAEF ALAE·SEBOSIA
               NAE OB · APRVM · EXIMIAE
               FORMAE · CAPTVM · QVEM·
                 MVLTI · ANTECESSO
               RES · EIVS · PRAEDARI ·
               NON POTVERVNT · V·S·L·P·
1041

'*Sacred to the Invincible Silvanus; Gaius Tetius Veturius Micianus, Commandant of Sebosius' Horse, set this up gladly in discharge of his vow, for the capture of a magnificent boar, which many of his predecessors had failed to bag.*'

V.S.L.P. = *voto solutus libenter posuit.*

This altar, with its memento of a Homeric episode in the career
of a pig-sticking cavalry officer, was found on Bollihope Common,
above Weardale; it was evidently set up miles from any human
habitation—probably cut on the spot—to mark the place where a
stern chase came to an end.

One of the shorter dedications to Silvanus may still be seen
built into a mediaeval wall at Lanercost Priory. It was dedicated
by a *collegium*—a club, in fact—of hunters.

162)   DEO · SANCTO

                       SILVANO   VE

                       N A T O R E S

                       B A N N I E S S

1905

'*To the holy god Silvanus, the Huntsmen of Banna (dedicate this).*'

BANNIESS = *Bannienses*; Banna is probably Bewcastle.

As to the occupations of the troops on winter evenings, or
when the weather was dreary, as it can be at some of those high
Whin Sill outposts, we can form a shrewd conjecture. Every
fort had, just outside the entrenchments, that necessity in Roman
eyes, a centrally-heated 'Turkish' bath-house, with hypocausts
under the floor. In a Northumberland winter, the bath-house
must have been about the only place where the Roman private
could be sure of getting and keeping decently warm, and no
doubt its rooms were crowded. It has been noticed that dedications to Fortune are particularly common close to the bath-houses.
The inference is obvious; one of the most important functions
of the regimental bath-house was to serve, incidentally, as the
regimental gambling-club.

For instance, this official dedication by a whole unit was found
in the bath-house at Aesica:

163)   DEAE   FORTV

                       VEXS · G · RETO

                       QVORVM CVR

                       AM AGIT TABE

                       LLIVS · VICTOR

                           ·Ↄ·

1724

'*To the Goddess Good Luck; (set up by) the Detachment of the Raetian Javelineers, under acting command of Tabellius Victor, Centurion.*'

VEXS·G·RETO = *Vexillatio Gaesatorum Retorum.*

A similar dedication comes from Habitancum, Risingham, an outpost a short march to the north, strongly garrisoned from the time of Severus (see next chapter).

164)

FORTVNAE·REDVC[I

IVLIVS · SEVERINVS

TRIB · EXPLICITO ·

BALINEO · V S L M

1212

'*To Fortune the Home-bringer, Julius Severinus, Tribune, on the completion of the bath-house, willingly and duly pays his vow.*'

And finally, one or two inscriptions must be quoted which show soldiers not unaffected by the scenery of unspoilt Tynedale and its moors. No doubt their feeling for it was not entirely Wordsworthian. Rather, it was the sense of the 'numinous', the sense that 'there is a deity in this place'; and yet, perhaps there is not so very much difference between this latter emotion and ours.

A dedication by German soldiers, from Carrawburgh:

165)

G E N I O

HVVS · LO

CI · TEXAND

ET · SVVE

VEX·COHOR

II NERVIOR

VM

1538

'*To the Spirit of this place; Texandrian and Suve ···? soldiers serving in a detachment of the Second Nervian Cohort (set this up).*'

HVVS of course = *huius.* A letter more or less matters little to these German tribesman. VEX. presumably = *vexillarii.*

Another by an officer, from Risingham—which lies, by the way, in a very beautiful position between the River Rede and the hills:

166)

· DIS · CVLTO
RIBVS·HVIV[S
LOCI · IVL ·
VICTOR·TRIB·

1208

'*To the Gods that inhabit this spot, Julius Victor, Tribune.*'

§3   HEALTH SERVICES
(*a*) MILITARY WATER-WORKS

167)

AQVA · ADDVCTA
ALAE · II · ASTVR ·
SVB·VLP·MARCELLO
LEG·AVG·PR·PR
(Chesters)

1463

168)

IMP   CAES   DIVI   SEVERI
NEPOS DIVI MAGNI ANTONINI F
M·AVREL·SEVERVS - - - - - - -
PIVS FELIX AVG PONTIF MAX
TRIB   POT   P   P   COS   AQVAM
VSIBVS MIL COH V GALLO IN
DVXIT CVRANTE MARIO VALERIANO
LEG EIVS PR PR
(South Shields)

1060

Every cohort-post had careful arrangements made for its water-supply. The reasons for this were, no doubt, severely military; but the presence of a copious supply of good water within the camp must have made a great difference to the amenity of frontier life. Inscriptions show that if there was not a good spring or well available close by, water might be brought from a distance. No. 167. The governor *may*, it is now thought, be a successor, perhaps grandson, of the earlier Marcellus (p. 109), since this regiment was definitely the third-century garrison here.

'*Water laid on for the Second Asturian Cavalry, under Ulpius Marcellus, Governor-General.*'

The stone formed part of the roof of the little aqueduct, and had been built in with the letters downwards. It was so found, quite unweathered, in modern times.

No. 168 is dated to the reign of that well-meaning but unfortunate young Emperor, Severus Alexander, 222-35 (see below, No. 205). He suffered official *damnatio memoriae* after his murder, and his last and distinguishing name has, according to the usual practice in such cases, been carefully chipped away:

'*The Emperor, Caesar, grandson of the deified Severus, son of Antoninus the Great, Marcus Aurelius Severus [Alexander] the Good, the Fortunate, Augustus, High Pontiff, holding the Tribunician Power, Father of his Country, Consul, laid on this water supply for the uses of the soldiers of the 5th Gallic Cohort, under the superintendence of Marius Valerianus his Governor-General.*'

'Antoninus the Great' perhaps signifies Septimius Severus' dynastic 'father', M. Aurelius.

(*b*) The Army Medical Service

All that we know of the doctors of the Roman army is told to us by the inscriptions, from which it appears that most of the 'doctors' were simply soldiers, who received extra pay in consideration of their skill. Their attentions may well have been rough and ready —'first aid', rather than scientific surgery and medicine; but by this arrangement it was possible at any rate for every unit to have its own medical orderlies. Epitaphs introduce us to two of these:

169)
```
              D·M
        A  N  I  C  I  O
        I N G E N V O
        M  E  D  I  C  O
        ORD   ·   COH
        I · T V N G R ·
            VIXIT·AN·XXV
```
1618; from Housesteads.

'*To the memory of Anicius Ingenuus, Doctor serving in the ranks of the 1st Tungrian Cohort; aged 25 years.*'

ORD· = *ordinarius*, 'serving in the ranks'.

170)

D   M

C·ACILIO BASSO

MEDIC · DUPLIC

COLLEGAE·EIVS

At Edinburgh, but the record of its place of origin is lost.

'*To the memory of Gaius Acilius Bassus, Doctor on double pay, his colleagues set up this stone.*'

DVPLIC· = *duplicarius*, 'receiving double a private's pay'. The stone is set up by the dead man's fellow-members of his *collegium*— that is, probably, his fellow-*duplicarii*; cf. No. 200.

However, the designation of a doctor as serving in the ranks seems to indicate that there were others who did not so serve. It is probably a higher-ranking physician who dedicates, in Greek, an altar to Asclepius, the Greek god or patron-hero of medicine, at Alauna (Ellenborough near Maryport) on the coast of Cumberland:

171)

Ἀσκληπιῷ

Α · Ἐγνάτιος·

808

Πάστορ ἔθηκεν

'*To Asclepius, Aulus Egnatius Pastor set this up.*'

§4   A CIVILIAN SETTLEMENT: VINDOLANDA

A little south of the Wall, near Housesteads and on the Stanegate, the Romans long kept one fort, Vindolanda ('Whitemeadow') at Chesterholm. Its civil settlement, a place of some industrial and local political importance, happens to be documented. The cohort in garrison was the 4th Gallic Part-Mounted, attested in numerous inscriptions.

172)

P R O · D O M V

DIVINA · ET · NV

MINIBVS · A V G

VSTORVM · V O L C

A N O · SACRVM

VICANI · VINDOL

ANDESSES · CVRAM

AGENTE · [- - -

1700

V   S   L   [M

'*For the Imperial House and the Divinities of the Augusti, Sacred to
Vulcan. The villagers of Vindolanda willingly and duly pay their vow.
- - - took charge of the work.*'

DOMV, *sic*. Vindolandesses, regular late Latin, intermediate
between classical -*enses* and Italian -*ese* (cf. No. 162: *venatores
Banniesses*).

We have here evidence of an organised *vicus*, such as we have
already seen on the frontier in Scotland. Since Vulcan, addressed
in a loyal vow for the imperial family by the community, seems
to be its chief god, we may infer a community of smiths and
perhaps coalminers; the Tyneside coal was then probably
accessible at and close to the surface, and coal was used quite
extensively in Britain. At nearby Housesteads, about a ton of it
was found still in store. The Cohort may have supervised the
work of smiths supplying weapons to the army, to see that they
did not supply them illegally to the wrong people.

The place may also have been the capital of an otherwise
unknown tribe; probably once members of the old Brigantian
confederacy:

173)   D E A E

                          S A I I A D A E

                          CVRIA   TEX

                          TOVERDORVM

                          V · S · L · M

1695

To the Goddess Saiiada (or *Sattada?*) *the Assembly of the Textoverdi
willingly and duly pay their vow.*

Saiiada or Sattada is equally unknown. The consonant-
combination -ST- or -XT-, as in Textoverdi, is alien to Celtic, and
when found in the name Corstopitum (Corbridge) in the *Antonine
Road-book*, has been supposed by experts to be corrupt. Conceiv-
ably it is a sound surviving in Britain from a pre-Indo-European
language.

The importance of Vindolanda accounts for a visit by an
official of the Governor of Britannia Superior (the Wall was in the
Lower province):

174)

```
        [DEO]SILVAN
        T   ·   AVRE
        LIVS  ·  MO
        DESTVS    B
        F   COS   PR
        OVINC I A E
        S VPER O R S
        LEG  II  AVG
```

1696

SVPERORS, *sic*; no doubt the i's of *Superioris* were indicated, ligatured to the r's, in paint.

'To the God Silvanus, *(dedicated by) Titus Aurelius Modestus, seconded on special duty by the Consular Governor of the Upper Province; soldier in Legion II Augusta.*'

And a member of the Consular Governor's bodyguard dies here:

175)

```
            D           M
        CORN · VICTOR · S · C
        MIL · ANN · XXVI · CIV
        PANN · FIL · SATVRNI
        NI·PP·VIX·AN·LV·D·XI
        CONIVX · PROCVRAVI
```

1713

'To the Spirits of the Dead. *Cornelius Victor*, singularis consularis, *served 26 years; a citizen of Pannonia; son of Saturninus, Leading Centurion. He lived 55 years and 11 days. His wife had this set up.*'

mil. here probably = *militavit.*

Singulares, as it were 'hand-picked', was an already ancient title for members of a general's guard. PP here most probably stands for *primipilaris*, giving the rank of Victor's father. If so, or even if not, if the other facts are as stated, it is a rather odd career. Victor joins the army rather late, and ends in a *corps d'élite* indeed, and pre-sumably doing clerical or light duties; but if his father was a *primipilaris*, almost of equestrian rank, the son has not done very well. As often in obituaries, one scents omissions.

Coniux procuravi: It would be attractive to render 'I, his wife'; but the third person is so stereotyped in such phrases, that one suspects a simple case of omission of the last letter, even though there is a blank space on the stone.

Vindolanda seems to have outlived the Roman government of Britain, to produce at least one fifth-century tombstone, in a time when to have one at all was the mark of a person of importance (see No. 234); but not long enough for its name, like that of Carlisle (Luguvalium, Caer Luel) to survive into English times. Vindolanda perished; the English called it 'the Roman fort at the field by the river', Chesterholm.

§5   THE DEPÔT TOWN: ROMAN CORBRIDGE

At the point where the great trunk road from York crossed the Tyne, Agricola planted a fort, to guard the bridge; a predecessor of the bridge whose foundations may still be seen in the bank of the river. On the site of this fort, later generals built a depôt with granaries and store-rooms of all kinds—an advanced base for the army on the frontier. And round the depôt grew up a busy little town of an area of some forty acres, whose name, written Corstopitum in the Antonine *Itinerary* but suspected of being corrupt,[1] survives in that of modern Corbridge, on the Cor Burn which here falls into the Tyne.

Roman Corbridge had a history of about 300 years, punctuated by disasters roughly coinciding with the ends of our centuries. A coin-hoard whose latest coin was of A.D. 98 dates a burnt stratum at the time of the first Roman withdrawal from Scotland; another was of 160 gold pieces, from Nero to Marcus Aurelius; a third of 48, of the fourth century, from Valentinian I to Magnus Maximus. These two correspond to two disasters which will be described in our next chapter. These cases, when people were killed or otherwise died without ever coming back to retrieve their buried savings, well illustrate the use of coin-hoards to date disasters.

Its inscriptions give a vivid impression of the town's varied life. To us it seems extraordinarily cosmopolitan, for a little place in a remote corner of the Empire; but a contemporary of St. Paul would not have been surprised. Were they not all Roman subjects? In the streets or market-place one might hear the languages of the eastern Mediterranean, as well as Latin and every dialect of the

---

[1] The -ST- is said to be un-Celtic. But cf. TEXTOVERDI in No. 173, from the same area?

west. Tungrian or Dacian infantry, Pannonian troopers, Syrian archers—they might come in parties to convoy grain back to their forts, or in twos and threes, on leave, to visit the nearest place where they could see 'life', a little less monotonous than at the posts 'up the line'. This is not mere imagination, for we have direct evidence of the presence, besides westerners and Italians, of Greeks, Phoenicians, Palmyrenes; traders, and priests of Oriental gods, all of whom must have made their living, directly or indirectly, out of the army. And besides the soldiers, there were the soldiers' wives and those veterans who chose to settle down near their old cantonments. They would all come into Corbridge if they had any special purchase to make—for a present, say, or a dedication to a god.

The gods that men worshipped here were equally varied. Roman Jupiter the Good and Great, and Syrian Jupiter Dolichenus; Persian Mithras, Tyrian Hercules, Sidonian Ashtoreth, British Brigantia, Spirit of the North-Country; we have dedications to them all; and in the later days there were Christians too, their presence attested by just one tiny inscription, the Greek Chi-Rho monogram, ⳩, that stands for the name of Christ, on a silver cup imported from abroad.

This way too will have come drafts of recruits, trudging thankfully over the bridge at the end of their march, to lie in the military lines overnight and leave next morning by the lateral road for the Wall. Sometimes there was a more than usual stir, when the Governor-General of Britain himself arrived with horsemen and legionaries, to deal by fighting or 'demonstration' with unrest in the north, and perhaps to leave a record of his coming in the shape of a dedication to the soldier's god. And this way too, but in the opposite direction, and leaving no mark in history, will have passed at times the Caledonian prisoners, dishevelled and in chains, into slavery.

First among the inscriptions may be placed a tombstone, dating from the earliest Roman campaigns in the north:

176)   DIS MANIBVS FLAVINVS
                 EQ ALAE PETR SIGNIFER
                 TVR CANDIDI AN XXV
                   STIP VII H S [E?

1172

The tombstone of a promising young cavalry soldier who died prematurely. The formula '*Hic situs est*' and the fact that the *ala* is not yet 'of Roman Citizens', an honour which they bear already in the diploma of A.D. 98, date it to the first century.

'*To the Gods of the Underworld. Here lies Flavinus, of Petreius' Horse, Ensign of Candidus' Troop, who died in the twenty-fifth year of his age and the seventh of his service.*'

The stone was used as building material in Hexham Abbey Church, where it now stands in one of the transepts; the inscription is cut below a fine relief; of the usual type, showing the ensign, in plumed helmet, trampling a barbarian under the feet of his horse. (It is sometimes explained locally as depicting the death of Flavinus; but this would be contrary to all Greek and Roman custom.)

The *ala Petriana* remained on the Wall for centuries, quartered at a place which came to be called Petriana after them: Stanwix, just across the river north of the civil town of Carlisle.

SOME DEDICATIONS:

177)

SOLI·INVICTO
VEXILLATIO
LEG·VI·VIC·P·F·F
SVB · CVRA · SEX ·
CALPVRN · AGRICO
LAE·LEG·AVG·PR·PR·

1137   Plate 4(*a*)

'*To the Sun-God, the Invincible, a detachment of Legion VI Victrix Pia Fidelis set this up, under the command of Sextus Calpurnius Agricola, Governor-General.*'

A dedication to Mithras, by his usual title, but without his oriental name; an early example of the official recognition of the soldiers' favourite religion, which ended, under the great soldier-Emperor Aurelian in the third century, by making a solar mono-theism the official religion of the State.

Calpurnius Agricola governed Britain about 161-4 under M. Aurelius and, as we are told by a historian, had to cope with a rebellion.

By kind permission of the Trustees of the Corbridge Excavation Fund

DEDICATIONS
(Nos. 177, 211)

Photo by Walter Scott, Bradford

Plate 4

178)

A P] O L L I N I
M A P O N O
· · · R N I V S
· · · · T R I B
D E D I C A V I T

1121

'To Apollo Maponus, Calpurnius (?) . . . ., Tribune, dedicated this.'

An officer's dedication to the classical Apollo, identified with the Celtic god Mapon, 'the Youth.' The stone, a fine one, but much damaged, once served as a base for Corbridge market-cross, at which period its top was hollowed out into a large socket.

179)

IOVI   AETERNO
DOLICHENO

ET   CAELESTI
B R I G A N T I A E
ET   ·   SALVTI

C · IVLIVS · AP
O L I N A R I S
⟩ LEG VI IVS DE

1131

'To Jupiter Dolichenus, Eternal; and to the Heavenly Spirit of the North-Country; and to Safety; Gaius Julius Apolinaris (sic), Centurion of the Sixth Legion, dedicates this by order of the gods.'

A centurion from York makes a dedication to an assortment of gods reminiscent of the Centurion of Auchendavy. IVS DE stands either for *iussus dedicavit* or *iussu deorum*. The stone seems to have had Apollinaris' name substituted for another; possibly the meaning is that Apollinaris felt it incumbent on him to dedicate an altar originally ordered by someone else, who may—for instance —have died before it was paid for.

The name of 'Heavenly Brigantia' is decorated with, on the left, a 'Genius' holding a cornucopia, and on the right a winged cupid with a bunch of grapes.

R.B.—K

180)
```
- - - - - -] ET
- - - -] NORVS
- - p] RAEP·CV
[H] ORR AGENS
           TEMPO
[R] E EXPEDITIO
NIS   FELICISSI
B R I T A N N I C
           V S L M
```

1143

'——— *quartermaster in charge of the Granaries, at the time of the
victorious British Campaign, pays his vow willingly and duly.*'

A fragment; more than half the stone is lost; but Haverfield
suggested with great probability that the dedicator gave his
position as '*Praepositus Curam Agens Horreorum*'—Quartermaster
of the Granaries; and certainly some such official must have been
one of the most important Romans in Corstopitum.

181)
```
ACT[AP]THC
BωMoNM
ECOPAC
ΠoΥΛΧεPM
ANεΘHKεN
```

1124

'*Thou seest me, an altar of Astarte; Pulcher set me up.*'

One of the most striking and amusing reminders extant of the
cosmopolitanism of the Roman Empire; an inscription forming a
Greek dactylic hexameter, dedicated, by a man bearing a Latin
name, to Astarte, Ashtoreth, the 'abomination of the Sidonians'
on the banks of the Tyne!

A companion altar to a Phoenician deity reads:

182)
```
HPAKΛεI
TΥPIω
ΔIoΔωPA
APXIεPεIA
```

1129

'*To the Tyrian Hercules, Diodora the High-Priestess.*'

This also is meant to be a hexameter, though with a most unclassical hiatus before *archiereia*.

These altars stood before twin temples, side by side. Since priests and priestesses were usually of the same sex as their deities, it looks as if Pulcher and Diodora, who may well have been husband and wife, set up altars to *each other's* divinities on settling down to what they doubtless hoped would be a profitable ecclesiastical career.

And once more, tombstones bring us into contact with some individuals:

BARATES OF PALMYRA

183)

            D]   M
BA] RATHES · PAL
MORENVS · VEXILA
VIXIT·ANOS·LXVIII

1171

'*To the memory of the Barathes of Palmyra, banner-maker(?), who lived 68 years.*'

As we possess the tombstone of the wife of a Barates (*sic*) of Palmyra, and as men of that famous Arabian oasis were not common on the Tyneside, though the name Barat(h)es *was* very common at Palmyra, it may be that we should identify the two.

VEXIL(L)A(rius) is interpreted either as 'flag-maker' or 'soldier in a detachment', and so 'veteran', since veterans awaiting discharge were often, according to Tacitus, retained under a *vexillum*. If the latter, he is different from the other Barates, who is clearly a rich man. (See No. 186.)

A LITTLE GIRL

184)

IVLIA   ·   MATER
NA · AN · VI IVL
M A R C E L L I N V S
FILIAE CARISSIMAE

1182

'*Here lies Julia Materna, aged six. Julius Marcellinus set this up to his beloved daughter.*'

An Unknown Soldier

185)   D · M
                     M I L E S
                      LEG II
                      [AVG]

1177

'*To the Spirits of the Departed. A soldier of Legion II Augusta.*'

This stone is broken at the bottom, but it is not likely that there was ever a name on it, since the name on a Roman tombstone invariably comes first. The stone may have marked the grave of a soldier whose body was recovered, long after, from the place where he fell.

§6   SOME INDIVIDUALS

This ends the Corbridge inscriptions; but some other individuals who lived and in most cases died on this frontier still deserve our notice.

Barates and his Wife

At South Shields was found a large and elaborate relief of a seated woman, with her jewel-box and her work-basket, and the inscription:

186)   DM·REGINA·LIBERTA·ET·CONIVGE·
              BARATES·PALMYRENVS·NATIONE·
              CATVALLAVNA·AN·XXX·

1065

'*To the Spirits of the Departed. To Regina, his freedwoman and wife; dedicated by Barates of Palmyra. (She was) of the Catuvellaunian tribe; aged 30.*'

Below, in Palmyrene script and language, is the legend: '*Regina, freedwoman of Barates. Alas!*'

Whether *Regina, liberta, coniuge,* and *Catuallauna* are all meant to be nominative or dative, this is a fine example of imperial 'vulgar Latin', in which the cases are in decay.

This stone gives us a whole character-sketch of this early representative of many Semites to make a fortune on Tyneside. Barates is well off, or he could not have afforded this sumptuous

monument. At the same time, he is no miser, or he *would* not have
afforded it. He is kindly too; for when he buys himself a British
woman slave, we find that before she died, still quite young, he
has set her free and made her his lawful wife. We notice too the
Semitic racial consciousness that leads him to add a line in his own
language, even in a place where everyone could read Latin and
very few could read Palmyrene.

Regina, since she has a tribe, was probably born free. Perhaps
she was left an orphan, with relatives who could not or would not
support her. But after experiencing the horror of being shipped
off for sale in the military area, *her* story at least has a happier
ending.

A Young Noble

187)

DEO · ANOCITICO ·
IVDICIIS · OPTIMO
RVM · MAXIMORVM
QVE·IMPP·N·SVB·VLP
MARCELLO COS · TINE
IVS · LONGVS · IN PRE
FECTVRA · EQVITVM
LATO·CLAVO·EXORNA
TVS ET · Q · D ·

1329

'*To the God Anociticus, dedicated by Tineius Longus, who, by the
decision of our best and greatest Emperors, has while serving as Praefect of
Cavalry, under Ulpius Marcellus, Consular Governor, been awarded the
Broad Stripe and appointed Quaestor.*'

Tineius Longus, serving as an equestrian cavalry officer,
receives the news that the joint Emperors—Marcus Aurelius and
Commodus, unless, as some think, the Governor is a second
Ulpius Marcellus under the Severi—have definitely given him the
hoped-for senatorial rank and quaestorship. He renders thanks
to a local god of the lower Tyne. His command was probably
that of the First Asturian Cavalry at Condercum, Benwell, where
the inscription was found.

IMPP N = *Imperatores nostri.*

The *latus clavus* or 'laticlave' was the broad purple stripe on the white tunic, which was the distinguishing mark of a senator.

QD = *quaestor designatus.*

A FREEDMAN

188)

D   ·   M

FELICIO · LIBERTI

V I X I T · A N N I S

XX

1290

'*To the memory of Felicio the freedman, who lived 20 years.*'

From Bremenium, High Rochester, in Redesdale; an ornamental tombstone, probably set up by the youth's former master.

The case of LIBERTI shows that FELICIO must be genitive too; it is therefore probably short for FELICIONIS.

A SLAVE

189)

*   *   *   *

*   *   *   *

HARDALIO

NIS

COLLEGIVM

CONSER

B · M · P ·

1436

From the shape of the stone, probably at least two lines are lost (R. P. Wright). We should probably read:

'(*Dis Manibus* . . .) *To* . . . , *slave of Hardalio. The Club of his fellow-slaves set this up to their well-deserving comrade.*'

From Hunnum (Halton Chesters). Copious evidence from other parts of the Empire shows that the Roman's desire to be at any cost properly buried was shared by his slaves; they therefore often came together in *collegia* like this one, burial societies which assured their members a funeral; they might develop into humble social clubs too.

CONSER (*vorum*, sc.).

B·M·P· = *Bene merenti posuit.*

A MOTHER

190)

```
      D      M      S
    AVR  ·  LVPV
    LE       MATRI
    P I I S S I M E
    D I O N Y S I V S
    F O R T V N A
    TVS  ·  FILIVS
        S         T
        T         L
```

1250

'*Sacred to the Gods of the Underworld. To Aurelia Lupula, his devoted Mother, Dionysius Fortunatus her son (set this up). Light lie the earth upon thee!*'

From Risingham. D·M·S = *Dis Manibus Sacrum*. S T T L stands for the verse tag '*Sit tibi terra levis*'.

A WIFE

191)

```
         D            M
    AVR  ·  T  ·  F  ·  AIAE
    D     ·     SALONAS
    AVR     ·     MARCVS
    Ɔ    OBSEQ    CON
    IVGI         SANCTIS
    SIMAE    QUAE    VI
    XIT   ANNIS   XXX
    SINE VLLA MACVLA
```

1828

'*To the Gods of the Underworld. To Aurelia Aia, Daughter of Titus, from Salonae; Aurelius Marcus, of the Century of Obsequens, (set this up) to his sainted wife, who lived for 33 years without stain.*'

From Carvoran. D = *Domo*. Salonae is Split in Dalmatia.

The fact that Aia is recorded explicitly as wife of a serving soldier dates this to the third century. It has been suggested that *sine ulla macula* 'has a Christian flavour'—especially since she comes from Salonae, where there was an early church. But (adds Mr Wright, *ad loc.*) 'the pagan use of the phrase is not unknown'.

Aurelius Marcus' name is of late type too. By the third century, the old Roman *praenomina*, too few to be distinctive in a large population, are rarely recorded in inscriptions. The *cognomen*, written last, becomes the sole personal name; but some of the old 'first names', among which Marcus is the commonest, continue in use *as* cognomina.

CHAPTER V

THE THIRD CENTURY AND AFTER

§1   THE AGE OF THE SEVERI (192-235)

Several inscriptions dating from the third century have been
quoted already in this book. In this chapter it remains to show
some of the epigraphic evidence, first on the work in Britain of
the dynasty founded by Severus, and then on some of the new
tendencies that transformed the Empire in the third century and
after.

Clodius Albinus

192)   A dedication from Rome:

Fortunae domesticae sanctae, aram pro salute et reditu L. Septimi Severi
Pertinacis Aug. [et D. Clodi] Septi [mi Albini Caesaris] L. Valerius
Frontinus, › Coh. II Vigil. sua pecunia posuit cum suis.

D 414

'To the holy goddess Fortune of the Home, for the safe return of the
Emperor Lucius Septimius Severus Pertinax [and of Decimus Clodius
Septimius Albinus Caesar], Lucius Valerius Frontinus, Centurion of the
Second Cohort of the Watch, set up this altar at his own charges, with his
family.'

The name of D. Clodius Albinus has been defaced, on this as
on other stones; but enough here remains for the rest to be
restored.

The Emperor Commodus, called Britannicus in honour of the
victories of his generals, was murdered, not undeservedly, in 192,
and two short-lived emperors followed. The Senate proclaimed
Helvius Pertinax, sometime governor of Britain, a second Galba,
who perished after a few months in a gallant but foredoomed
attempt to restore discipline in the Praetorian Guard. The
Guards then held their famous auction of the Empire, which was

bought by Didius Julianus, elderly, very distinguished, and the richest man in Rome. But just as when Otho suborned the Guards and murdered Galba a hundred and twenty years before, so now the frontier armies refused to bow before the nominee of the palace troops, and proclaimed each their own general: Pescennius Niger in the east, Severus on the Danube, Clodius Albinus in Britain. Each seems to have been a not unworthy choice. Niger was perhaps the most able of the three; Albinus, the secret hope of the senate, the most cultured and attractive; Severus was probably the most forcible character. Also he was nearest to Rome, and had the strongest army.

Severus secured the capital and the execution of Didius, 'recognised' Albinus, and marched against Niger, whom, not without difficulty, he defeated and killed. It is probably to these months that our inscription belongs: the 'safe return' of the Emperor, for which our Centurion of Police prays, must be from the campaign against Pescennius. The Governor of Britain was not taking part in this campaign, but as Severus had formally conferred on him the rank of Caesar or junior Emperor, the dedicator feels it correct to name him. The inscription confirms literary evidence that Clodius was for a time recognised as Caesar.

But Severus probably never meant to leave him long. The Roman world was not large enough for him and a rival. A breach soon came, and in 197 Albinus was defeated and killed in a desperate battle near Lyons.

SEVERUS IN BRITAIN

Naturally the results in Britain were disastrous. The frontier was left weakly held; there was invasion from the north, rebellion in the hill country, widespread destruction of the hated forts; and the defeated army, sent back with diminished numbers and shattered morale, was unequal to its task. The new governor, Virius Lupus, though he won some successes, felt compelled to win a respite by buying off the barbarian attacks.

An altar from north Yorkshire shows us the troops under Lupus engaged, not surprisingly, in the restoration of burnt-out buildings:

193)

DAE·FORTVNAE   (*sic*)
VIRIVS · LVPVS
LEG·AVG·PR·PR
BALINEVM · VI
IGNIS · EXVST
VM·COH·I THR
ACVM · RESTI
TVIT · CVRAN
TE · VAL · FRON
TONE · PRAEF
EQ·ALAE·VETTO

730

'To the Goddess Fortune. *Virius Lupus*, Legatus Augusti pro praetore, *restored this bath-house destroyed by fire for the First Thracian Cohort. Valerius Fronto, officer commanding the Vettonian Cavalry Regiment, supervised the work.*'

For dedications to Fortune in or at bath-houses, cf. No. 163, etc. The fort at Bowes, Roman Lavatrae or Lavarae ('Laughing Water'?) lies on the road over the Pennines from Catterick to Carlisle, now A66. It was long garrisoned by this once Thracian Battalion. That it is the colonel of the Vettonian Horse, a more senior officer, commanding at Vinovia (Binchester) on the road due north from Catterick, who had his name commemorated, must mean that he was in general command of the area. The First Thracians were probably temporarily without a *praefectus*.

The history of these years marks the onset of the disease of civil war between the professional soldiers and consequent weakness on the frontiers, which was to undermine the strength of the whole Empire in the following century. The character of Severus too was typical of the coming age; a north African who spoke his Latin with an accent, he was, though by no means uneducated, the least Roman of all who had yet occupied the throne of the Caesars. But he was a soldier and a ruler, and at last in response to repeated unfavourable reports he came over in person.

A dedication from Greetland, near Halifax, dated 208, commemorates these campaigns:

On front:

194)

D   VICT   BRIG
ET NVM A/A/GG
T AVR AVRELIAN
VS D D PRO SE
ET SVIS S MAG

On side:

AN T O N I N [O
III ET GETA [II
627   COS

'To the Goddess Brigantia Victory and to the Divinity of the Emperors, Titus Aurelius Aurelianus gave and dedicated this offering for himself and his, when he himself was Master of Ceremonies.

'Third consulship of Antoninus and second of Geta.'

D VICT BRIG = *Deae Victoriae Brigantiae*. This personification of the North-Country becomes popular at this time.

NVM A/A/GG = *Numini Augustorum*.

D D = *Dedit, dedicavit*, and S MAG, it is thought, = *se magistro*.

The Consuls for 208 were Severus' sons, the elder, nicknamed Caracalla (a Gallic word meaning a heavy cloak—'Ulster'), who bore the honoured names of Marcus Aurelius Antoninus, being associated with his father as Augustus, while Geta, the younger, had to be content with the rank of Caesar.

By this time the Emperor and his sons had arrived with power-ful reinforcements, and a long list of large and imposing inscrip-tions from the wall and its supporting stations show that the frontier was thoroughly restored and strengthened. In this whole area there began a period of reconstruction and rebuilding that continued during the next twenty-five years.

One of the earliest comes from Habitancum, Risingham, in Redesdale, one of several strong outposts established or re-established by Severus north of the Wall. It is a little damaged at the top, but the Emperor's titles can be inserted from other inscriptions. It remains a fine and ornate slab, though the style of writing, with its numerous ligatured letters—e.g. POЯTAΛ for PORTAM—compares unfavourably, to our eyes, with the clear bold lettering of a hundred years before. The inscription is enclosed within a large wreath of conventionalised leaves and berries, while to the left and right stand the figures of Mars and Victory.

195)

[IMP CAES L
SEPT SEVERO PIO PERTIN
ACI ARAB ADI]AB. PARTH[I]CO MAXI.
COS. III. ET M. AVREL. ANTONINO PIO
COS. II AVG. [ET P. SEPT. GETAE, NOB.CAES.]
PORTAM CVM MVRIS VETVSTATE DI
LAPSIS IVSSV ALFENI SENECIONIS V. C.
COS., CVRANTE OCLATINIO ADVENTO PROC.
AVGG. NN. COH I VANGION. M. EQ.
CVM AEM[I]L SALVIANO TRIB.
SVO A SOLO REST.

1234   Plate 5

'In honour of the Emperor Lucius Septimius Severus Pius Pertinax Arabicus Adiabenicus Parthicus Maximus, Thrice Consul, and of Marcus Aurelius Antoninus Pius, Twice Consul, Augustus, and of Publius Septimius Geta the noble Caesar, this gate with its walls, which had fallen through lapse of time, was by order of His Excellency Alfenus Senecio, Consular Governor, and under the superintendence of Oclatinius Adventus, Procurator of Their Majesties, Restored from ground-level by the First Cohort of Vangiones, 1000 strong, part-mounted, under Aemilius Salvianus, Tribune in Command.'

Of the emperor's imposing array of titles, Pertinax shows that he declared himself the avenger and legitimate successor of his unfortunate predecessor, while Pius, and the official style of his elder son, marks his 'heraldic' claim to descent from the revered Antonines. Adiabene, whence another of his titles, lies in the mountainous regions south of the Caucasus, invaded by Severus during his Parthian wars.

The two consulships of Caracalla fix the date between 205 and 208.

The obliteration of the name of Geta, like that of Clodius Albinus in No. 192, is deliberate. The brothers were not friends, and shortly after their father's death Caracalla succeeded in making away with Geta. The victim's memory was then, of course, officially damned, and his name more or less successfully erased from monuments in all parts of the Empire.

VETVSTATE DILAPSIS is a piece of official 'eye-wash'. No Roman inscription, commemorating the restoration of military buildings, ever admits that the reason why they needed repairing was enemy action (cf. No. 223).

V.C.COS = *viri clarissimi consularis*. *Vir clarissimus* was at this time the regular title of high officers of senatorial rank.

AVGG· NN. = *Augustorum Nostrorum*.

A SOL. REST = *a solo restituit*.

From 208 to 210 Severus and the young Antoninus warred in Caledonia. The historians Dio and Herodian tell us in vague terms of laborious campaigns in wet country, with much bridging of bogs and tidal firths, at the end of which Severus 'drew near to the furthest end of the island'. Dio adds that he suffered appalling losses from the climate and the guerilla tactics of the Caledonians; probably unfairly, for civilian senators, of whom Dio was one, were hostile to the memory of Severus and his regime, based nakedly on the army.

Archaeology adds a great deal to our knowledge. A huge series of granaries at South Shields (Arbeia of the *Notitia*), at least twenty in number, could have held grain for three months for 40,000 men; and in them were found many lead seals with the heads of Severus and his sons and the lettering AVGG, 'Of the Two Augusti'. So, when we find that the only two places in Scotland showing intensive Severan occupation are Cramond on the Forth and a large base at Carpow, on the north shore of the Firth of Tay, we may conclude that Severus avoided a laborious march across the hostile Lowlands by transporting all his supplies and perhaps most of his infantry too to mid-Scotland by sea, to strike directly at the proud Caledonians in their highlands. From thence, among the temporary 'marching camps' which lie at intervals up to the Moray Firth (several of them discovered in recent years by Dr K. St. Joseph's air photography), a series of the largest size, no less than 120 acres, is thought to belong to this massive expedition. It was carefully and imaginatively planned, repeating Agricola's strategy, care for supplies and use of sea-power, on a far larger scale. The emphasis on roads and bridges is also illustrated by a coin-type of Caracalla as Antoninus Augustus, Cos. III (after 208), showing an army crossing a bridge of boats, with the legend TRAIECTVS.

During the winters, as under Agricola, a bridgehead was held on the Tay; but this time, down on the Firth. Carpow already in Ptolemy's geography seems to bear the name Orrea; read Horrea, 'Granaries'; and Ptolemy's information derives from Agricola's campaigns. It was now reoccupied. Here R. E. Birley (E. B. *filius*) in 1961-62 made important discoveries: a fort (not camp) of the exceptional area of 32 acres, dated by pottery and, most exactly, by two coins in mint condition, struck in 205-8. Over 200 stamped tiles identified the garrison, or the legionary component of it. Two of these, unbroken, bear the interesting legend:

196)   LEG·VI VIC·B·P·F·
JRS LIII (1963), pp. 127, 164 and plate XVII

The letter B, additional to the legion's well-known titles, probably indicates the new 'full style' LEGIO VI VICTRIX BRITAN-NICA PIA FIDELIS.

The fort is large enough for half a legion. Probably we should imagine it as garrisoned by a *vexillatio* of 1,000 or 2,000, plus *auxilia*.

Through all this too, even in war, Romans and Caledonians were beginning to discover each other as human beings. Dio mentions an interview between the wife of Argentocoxus, a Caledonian chief, and the wife of Severus, the powerful Syrian Empress Julia Domna, 'Mother of the Army' as she was officially styled. We do not know who Argentocoxus was; he may have been an exile who had fled to the Romans. But failing complete conquest, some kind of political understanding was becoming possible.

And the conquest did fail. For all its efficiency in building, road-making and organisation of supplies, the Roman army was perhaps growing too ponderous; and there is no evidence that it ever operated beyond the Highland line. Severus thought in 210 that he had obtained submission; but as soon as the main army had retired south for the winter, hostility showed itself again, even among the Maeatae (the new name of the people of mid-Scotland). Severus breathed threats of wholesale depopulation; but he was 65 years old, and early in 211 he died at York. Caracalla, whose villainy and worthlessness are perhaps over-emphasised by the historians, was anxious to get back to Rome, as he well might be for political reasons. He made a treaty, stigmatised as dishonourable by the writers, and withdrew the troops from Cramond and Carpow.

During these campaigns the issue of coins with the legend VICTORIAE BRIT. was only to be expected; coins were the greatest propaganda medium of the empire. But that the empire in general was taking notice of the British War is shown also by local loyal inscriptions; for instance, from Gigthis in Severus' native Africa:

197)

V I C T O R I A E
B R I T T A N I C A E
IMPPP·L·SEPTIMI SEVE
RI PII PERTINACIS ET
M · AVRELI ANTONINI
[ET·P·SEPTIMI GETAE]
AVGG[G]·GIGTHENSES

D 436   P V B L I C E

'*In honour of the Victory in Britain of our Three Emperors, the Augusti Lucius Septimius Severus Pius Pertinax, Marcus Aurelius Antoninus [and Publius Septimius Geta] the People of Gigthis (set this up) at the Public Cost.*'

Geta's name is erased as usual; and, for good measure, the third G of AVGGG.

These claims of victory were not entirely empty. Severus' frontier was the most durable that Roman Britain ever had. It lasted, essentially unchanged, for over 150 years. But the essential defeat is shown by the fact that that frontier still had to be left heavily manned.

Many inscriptions show this, both on the Wall and (very conspicuously) in Severus' new outposts. Fragments of a huge text, originally occupying five slabs, from Risingham (*RIB* 1235), show, in addition to the 1st Vangiones, a detachment of Raeti Gaesati, Raetian Javelin-men (cf. No. 163, above) and a special company of local Scouts, *Exploratores Habitancenses*. Altogether, the officer in command there had about 1500 men, a balanced force: the regular infantry and cavalry of the double-size cohort, the light-armed Raetians and the Scouts whose business was to

INSCRIPTION IN HONOUR OF SEVERUS
(No. 195)

By kind permission of the Society of Antiquaries of Newcastle-upon-Tyne

Plate 5

know every gully of the moors, and all that went on there. And Habitancum was not even in the very front line.

One short inscription, on a votive altar set up by the Raetians, is still seen to be built into a staircase at Jedburgh Abbey, whither it was taken with many wagon-loads of other stones—probably from the near-by Roman outpost of Cappuck, rather than all the way across the Cheviots—when the Abbey was building in the middle ages:

198)
IOM VE[X
ILATIO RETO
RVM GAESA
Q · C · A IVL
SEVER · TRIB

2117
'*To Jupiter the Good and Great, the Detachment of Raetian Javelineers under Julius Severinus, Tribune (dedicate this altar).*'

Q·C·A = *quorum curam agit.*

Another similarly powerful post was established at the old fort of Bremenium, High Rochester, also in Redesdale, a short march further north along the Dere Street, the old Antonine road. Here too the garrison was a *cohors milliaria equitata,* a double-strength cohort with a contingent of cavalry:

199)
IMP · CAES · M · AVRELIO
SEVERO · ANTONINO
PIO · FELICI · AVG · PARTHIC
MAX · BRIT · MAX · GERM
MAX · PONTIFICI · MAXIM
TRIB · POTEST · XVIIII · IMP · II
COS · III · PROCOS · P · P · COH · I
FIDA·VARDVL·C·R·EQ·∞·ANTO
NINIANA·FECIT·SVB·CVRA · · · ·
· · · · · · · LEG · AVG · PR · PR ·

1279
'*In honour of the Emperor Marcus Aurelius Severus Antoninus the Good, the Fortunate, (surnamed) Parthicus Maximus, Britannicus Maximus, Germanicus Maximus, Pontifex Maximus, in the nineteenth year of his Tribunician Power, twice saluted Imperator, thrice Consul, Proconsul, Father of his Country: the Emperor's Own First Loyal Vardullians,*'

R.B.—L

Roman Citizens, part-mounted, 1000 strong, erected this, under the orders of ——, Governor-General of His Majesty.'

Here the name of a governor has been damned and obliterated. ∞ = M, = *Milliaria.*

The date is 216. Caracalla's *Tribunicia Potestas* is reckoned from his first proclamation as Augustus in 198.

At Bremenium too we find a company of local *Exploratores* in addition to the Cohort. An altar shows them conscientiously Romanising, with the encouragement of the Commandant:

200)
```
            D        R         S
            DVPL · N · EXPLOR
            BREMEN     ·    ARAM
            I N S T I T V E R V N T
            N · EIVS · C · CAEP
            CHARITINO      TRIB
1270        V · S · L · M ·
```

'Sacred to the Goddess Roma.

'The double-pay men of the Numerus *of Bremenian Scouts set up this altar on her birthday, under the superintendence of Caepio Charitinus, Tribune, paying their vow willingly and duly.'*

An official dedication by, as it were, the Sergeant's Mess of the Scouts. *Duplicarii* included such 'NCOs' as the medical orderlies (cf. No. 170), the *signifer* and the *tesserarius*, a kind of orderly-sergeant, who received the watchword of the day on a tablet, the *tessera*, for transmission to the ranks.

D.R.S. = *Deae Romae Sacrum;* N in line 4, probably NATALI (the Birthday of Rome, April 21st). C = *curante.*

And later:

201)
```
            G · D · N · ET
            S  I  G  N  O  R  V  M
            COH · I · VARDVL[L
            ET · N · EXPLORA
            TOR · BREM · GOR
            EGNAT      ·      LVCILI
            ANVS · LEG AVG PR PR
            CVRANTE        CASSIO
1262        S A B I N I A N O  T R I B
```

'To the Divinity of our Emperor and of the Standards of the First Vardullian Cohort and of the Emperor Gordian's Own Company of Bremenian Scouts Egnatius Lucilianus, His Majesty's Governor-General (set up this altar), by the agency of Cassius Sabinianus, Tribune.'

G·D·N· in line 1 = *Genio Domini Nostri.* N, in line 4, = *numerus.*

This dedication of an altar to the 'Spirits of the Standards' of two units, in association with that of the Emperor, by the *Legatus Augusti Pro Praetore* himself, looks like a compliment to the regiments for some piece of valued service—as the grant of the name of the Emperor Gordian (238-44) to the Bremenian Scouts certainly is.

Work on the Severan frontier went quietly on, through the reign of Caracalla, and through those of his short-lived successors. About 217-19 a certain Modius Julius was governor, and two inscriptions naming him show the Army of Britain little disturbed by the assassination of Caracalla in 217 by his praetorian prefect Macrinus, or that of Macrinus in the following year, when the dynasty of Severus was restored in the person of yet another Marcus Aurelius, better known to infamy as Elagabalus.

One of Modius' inscriptions is a fine slab, adorned with a sabre to right of the lettering and a palm-branch to left, found beside the main west gate at Birdoswald—Camboglanna, a Celtic name meaning 'Twisted Glen.'

202)

SVB MODIO IV
LIO LEG AVG PR ·
PR COH·I·AEL DC·
CVI PRAEEST M
CL   MENANDER
TRIB·

1914

'Under Modius Julius, His Majesty's Governor-General (this gateway was restored) by the 1st Hadrian's Own Dacian Cohort, commanded by Marcus Claudius Menander, Tribune.'

The Greek cognomen of the Tribune is a sign of the times; this is one of the first appearances in the commissioned ranks of the army in Britain of men from the Greek-speaking east, which becomes increasingly common.

Modius' other appearance is at Netherby, Castra Exploratorum

of the Antonine Road-Book, ten miles north of Carlisle; the stone
purports to show a large working party, including drafts from
two legions, establishing an outpost in advance of the west end of
the wall of nearly the same size as, and corresponding to,
Habitancum and Bremenium in the east. But it is on sandstone,
which has weathered badly, and an attempt to recut it has not
improved matters. Haverfield made out the first half of it as
follows:

203) *Imp. Caes. M. Aur. Antonino p. f. cos. II, vexil. leg. II Aug. et
XX. v. v., item coh. I Ael. Hisp. ∞. eq., sub cura Modi Juli leg. Aug.
pr. pr., instante Ael · · · .*
RIB 980 and Plate XV

'*In the second consulship of the Emperor Marcus Aurelius Antoninus the
Good and Fortunate, detachments of Legions II Augusta and XX Valeria
Victrix, and the 1st (Hadrian's Own) Spanish Cohort, 1000 strong
part-mounted, under Modius Julius, His Majesty's Governor-General,
and under the superintendance of Aelius - - - -*'

Mr Wright however deprecates placing any reliance on this.

Finally, the new scheme of 'defence in depth' was completed
by an outpost at Bewcastle, Banna, opposite the left centre of the
Wall—seven miles north of Camboglanna by a dead straight
Roman road, about fifteen east of Netherby, and some twenty
miles in a straight line across the boggy moors, a little south of
west from Habitancum. A few dedications by commanders there
show by their phrases and lettering their third-century date; for
instance:

204) DEO SANCTO COCIDIO
      Q   PELTRASI[V]S
      MAXIMVS   TRIB
      EX CORNIC VLARIO
      PRAEFF PR[A]ETORIO EE
      M M V V V S L M

989

'*To the holy god Cocidius, Quintus Peltrasius Maximus, Tribune,
ex-clerk to their Eminences the Praetorian Prefects, pays his vow
willingly and duly.*'

A former staff-sergeant in the praetorian headquarters at Rome (a post which frequently led to promotion to equestrian rank) 'willingly and duly pays'—no doubt on taking up his first independent command—a vow, perhaps to dedicate an altar to the Gods of the Place, wherever he might be stationed, if the coveted promotion should be given to him.

EEMMVV = *eminentissimorum virorum*, the regular honorific title of the praetorian prefects under the later empire, as was *vir clarissimus* of senators. The letters are doubled, like the F of PRAEF(*ectorum*), to indicate the dual number; cf. AVGGG for 'the three Augusti' in No. 197, etc.

Last in this series of rebuilding inscriptions are some from the reign of the last Severus, the virtuous but insufficiently strong-handed Alexander. Some of these show the troops, their fortifications perfected, now undertaking other ambitious, if less immediate, tasks. Waterworks have already been noticed (No. 168). A stone from Netherby shows the Cohors Aelia Hispanorum building a riding-school (*baselica* [sic] *equestris exercitatoria*); one from Great Chesters, Aesica, a granary. This is dated to 'the consulship of Fuscus'—A.D. 225:

205)

```
IMP · CAES · M · AVR · SEVE
RVS · ALEXANDER · P · FEL
AVG  ·  HORREVM  ·  VETV
STATE · CONLABSVM · MIL
COH · II · ASTVRVM · S · A ·
A · SOLO · RESTITVERVNT
PROVINCIA · REGENTE [· · ·
MAXIMO LEG [AVG PR PR CVR?
VAL MARTIA [LE Ɔ LEG · · ?
F]VS[CO II ET DEXTRO COS?
```

1738

'*The Emperor Marcus Aurelius Severus Alexander, the Good, the Fortunate, Augustus. The soldiers of the 2nd Asturian Cohort, Severus Alexander's Own, restored this granary, fallen through age, in the governorship of · · · Maximus, [under the superintendence of] Valerius Marti[alis, centurion of the · · · Legion, in the consulship of F]us[cus for the second time and Dexter].*'

Normally in such inscriptions the Emperor is made grammatical subject of the verb 'restored' or the like, and the text continues 'by

the agency of the soldiers of such-and-such a unit'; or else, if the
unit is made subject, the Emperor's name and titles are given in
the dative: 'In honour of the Emperor ——, the —— Cohort
erected this.' Here, the Emperor's name stands without grammatical construction, and the text begins again 'The soldiers . . .
etc., restored.' It is a minor piece of slovenliness in drafting,
which a second-century Roman officer would scarcely have
'passed'.

MIL = *milites.*

S·A· = *Severiana Alexandriana.*

PROVINCIA·REGENTE = *provinciam regente.*

The date depends on the restoration of the last line, assuming
that this Fuscus is identical with the only one known to have been
consul during Alexander's reign. Collingwood notes: 'The slab is
in fresh condition but purposely broken. It was evidently taken
down when the Emperor suffered *damnatio memoriae* after his
death.' He was murdered by his troops on the Rhine in 235.

A bronze votive tablet, eight inches by three and five-eighths,
found at Colchester, perhaps shows the Romans again harbouring
a 'political exile':

206)   DEO · MARTI · MEDOCIO · CAMP
                 ESIVM · ET · VICTORIE · ALEXAN
                 DRI · PII · FELICIS · AVGVSTI · NOSI
                 DONVM · LOSSIO · VEDA · DE · SVO
                 POSVIT·NEPOS·VEPOGENI·CALEDO

191

'*To the God Mars Medocius of the Lowlanders* (?) *and to the Victory of
our Emperor Alexander the Good and Fortunate, Lossio Veda the
Caledonian, of the clan of Vepogenus, dedicated this gift at his own cost.*'

The spelling NOSI for *Nostri* is no doubt phonetic; it suggests,
further, that CAMPESIVM is a similar simplification of *campestrium*,
'plain-dwellers'.

VICTORIE for *victoriae* is regular 'vulgar Latin'.

NEPOS, it has been suggested, may not be the Latin word
meaning 'grandson', but a similar Celtic word, without a Latin
equivalent, meaning some tribal division—'clan' or 'sept'; cf.
No. 235 below.

§2 THE LATER THIRD CENTURY:
FROM VALERIAN TO CONSTANTIUS

Valerian and Gallienvs, and the Imperivm Galliarvm

The middle years of the third century were a time of disaster. Assassination followed assassination. From 211 onwards, ten Augusti so perished in thirty-eight years. This did not necessarily matter except to the persons immediately concerned; but respect for the imperial office could not but decay. Simultaneously the discipline of the army was impaired by the repeated demonstrations that the civil administration was impotent as soon as the soldiers chose to disobey it.

The result of all this was seen when the Empire was at last threatened by really formidable foes without—the Goths, driven on by the Huns, and the rejuvenated Persia of the Sassanid dynasty. In 249 the Emperor Decius was defeated and killed in a desperate turning-at-bay of the Goths, whom he had been in a fair way to drive in flight out of the Balkan provinces; in 260, Chosroes the Persian made the Emperor Valerianus prisoner and captured Antioch. Under these blows the Empire broke into fragments. By 265 Gallienus, son of Valerian, ruled only Italy and the central provinces; the east had passed under the Syrian prince of Palmyra; Franks and Alemanni raided Gaul and Italy; and the western provinces with the Rhine and British armies— now locally recruited—declined to obey a central government that was for ever calling for men and money for wars further east.

Hence arose the Empire of the Gallic Lands, which in its fifteen years of life justified its existence, at least locally. The armies there proclaimed their own trusted generals *Imperatores*; and under the valiant Postumus (259-69) enemies were held at bay more effectively than were those further east by Gallienus.

The inscriptions of Britain show that this island acknowledged the rule of the Gallic emperors. They show too that during this turmoil Britain almost alone among the provinces was apparently at peace. Severus had done his work well; and inscriptions refer to such routine matters as the repair of buildings and the upkeep and extension of the roads.

New Buildings at Caerleon

207)   IMPP· VALERIANVS · ET · GALLIENVS

AVGG · ET · VALERIANVS · NOBILISSIMVS

CAES · COHORTI · VII · CENTVRIAS · A   SO

LO   RESTITVERVNT · PER · DESTICIVM   IVBAM

VC · LEGATVM · AVG · PR · PR · ET

VITVLASIVM · LAETINIANVM · LEG · LEG

II · AVG · CVRANTE · DOMIT · POTENTINO

PRAEF · LEG · EIVSDEM ·

334

A large slab from the legionary camp.

'The *Emperors Valerianus and Gallienus, the Augusti, and Valerianus, the noble Caesar, restored from ground-level the company-barracks of No. VII Cohort, by the agency of His Excellency Desticius Juba, Imperial Governor-General, and Vitulasius Laetinianus, Officer Commanding Legion II Augustam and through the superintendence of Domitius Potentinus, Quartermaster of that Legion.*'

The Caesar is the elder Valerian's younger son.

The governor of (Upper) Britain, we notice, bears a Punic *cognomen*, Ayub or Job; the same as the name of that King Juba of Numidia who fought against Caesar for the Pompeians.

VC = *vir clarissimus*, cf. No. 195.

The 'Prefect of the Legion' was in earlier days called 'Prefect of the Camp'; he was the officer, usually a promoted senior centurion, responsible for a large camp's internal economy, and so corresponds generally to a quartermaster. Since the days of Domitian every legion had a separate permanent camp, so that the Prefect came to be called Prefect of the Legion.

Two Milestones

'Milestones', giving the Emperor's names and titles, seem in the third century to have become a standard form of loyal dedication. Of 96 recorded in *RIB* I, 92 belong to the age from Severus to Constantine II (337-40). Few of them, in fact, actually give any mileage. The following, among others, commemorate the *Imperium Galliarum*:

208)

IMP DO
N MAR
CASSIA
NIO LATINIO
P O S T V M O
PIO FEL AVG

2260

'In honour of our Lord the Emperor Marcus Cassianius Latinius Postumus, the Good, the Fortunate, Augustus.'

From Trecastle Hill, on the Roman road 14 miles west of Brecon.

209)

IMP CAES
MARCO
PIAONIO
VICTORI
NO PF INV
AVG PONT
M A X
TR P · P P
A·L·S·M
P · X · IIII

2241

'To the Emperor Caesar Marcus Piaonius Victorinus, the Good, the Fortunate, the Unconquered, Augustus, High Pontiff, holding the Tribunician Power, Father of his Country. From Lindum to Segelocum, 14 miles.'

From Lincoln.

DO N in No. 208 = *domino nostro*: INV, in No. 209 = *invicto*: L stands for *Lindo*: S for Segelocum, Littleborough, on the Trent.

Victorinus was the successor of Postumus. This provincial Caesar Augustus copies closely the official style of a first-century *princeps*.

THE LAST GALLIC CAESAR

An altar from Birdoswald and a few milestones commemorate, in turn, Victorinus' successor:

210)

I   O   M
COH · I · AEL D[A]C
T E T R I C I ANORV
M C P POMP[ON
I]VS D · · · · · · · ·
RAT · · · · · · · · · ·
T · · · · · · · · · · · ·

1885

'*To Jupiter the Good and Great (this altar is dedicated by) the First Aelian Cohort of Dacians, Emperor Tetricus' Own, under Pomponius (?) Desideratus . . . . , the Tribune . . . . . . ?*'

The c p in line 4 stands for *cui praeest*.

Tetricus' reign was short. The great Illyrian soldier-Emperor Aurelian, having reconquered the east and captured Palmyra, moved against him (273). Tetricus' German and British legions were eager to fight, but their leader thought it prudent to make a private arrangement with Aurelian, and the Gallic Empire ended, not with an emperor deserted by his troops, but with an army deserted in the day of battle by the emperor for whom it was fighting. He served later in civil posts under Aurelian.

TENDENCIES IN THE THIRD CENTURY

On the whole, then, Britain prospered throughout the third century. 'Roman villas'—the manor-houses of the civilised British gentry—appear to have been more numerous and the towns larger in A.D. 270 and again in 300, and in 330, than they had been before. Among inscriptions dealing with British affairs, those which show us the career of a British centurion (No. 74), the local council of the Silures at Caerwent (No. 67), the business dealings of a merchant of York and Lincoln with Bordeaux (No. 65), all date from this century. But the inscriptions show also some ominous signs of decline. Emperors and high officials adopt ever more pretentious titles, but the inscriptions in which these appear are less well cut than those of the Antonine age, and resort much to ligatured letters, economising at the expense of the reader. And after the middle of the century far fewer people, and on far fewer occasions, choose, or can afford, to set up inscriptions at all. Amid the wars and turmoil, the Empire is growing poorer and less literate; with all that that implies with regard to breadth of outlook upon life in general.

Among barbarian soldiers who still *do* set up inscriptions, we may remember Notfried and the other Valkyrie-worshippers at Housesteads (Nos. 146-8).

Another tendency, the orientalisation even of the west of the Empire, is neatly illustrated by a dedication at York:

Serapis at York

211)
<pre>
DEO · SANCTO
SERAPI
TEMPLVM·A·SO
LO·FECIT
CL · HIERONY
MIANVS · LEG
LEG · VI · VIC
</pre>

658   Plate 4(*b*)

'*To the Holy God Serapis, this Temple was built from its foundation, by Claudius Hieronymianus, General Officer Commanding Legion VI Victrix.*'

This stone is well cut, without ligatured letters; the date, probably early in the century. The dedicator's surname tells a tale; based on the Greek Hieronymos, it has been 'naturalised' in Latin by the addition of the termination -anus. A parallel case is that of the Emperor Diocletian; originally an Illyrian soldier named Docles, he first Grecised his name, Diocles or Diocletos, and then further embellished it into the resonant Roman formation Diocletianus.

The cult of Serapis (Osiris-Apis) was a 'salvationist' religion like Mithraism and Pauline Christianity. It had been popular since the days of the early Ptolemies in the Hellenistic east; but what would Tacitus have thought of a *legatus legionis* who publicly professed this sort of thing?

British Troops on the Continent

So secure, indeed, was the peace in Britain—whereas on the Rhine the ominous names of Franks and Alemanni appear—that British troops could be detached to deal with a revolt in Brittany, Armorica, a kind of *jacquerie* of which we hear from the literary sources; it was a movement of despair on the part of peasants ground down by taxation in the government's effort to support its wars and swollen armies. A long sepulchral inscription records the career of a centurion who rose to equestrian rank, and who, while serving as quartermaster-general at York, was given charge of a task-force against the Bacaudae, as these rebels were called. The style of the lettering suggests the third century. The name

Artorius, by the way, is that which, it has been suggested, may later have been borne by the sub-Roman *dux*, Arthur.

212)

D. M. L. Artorius Castus › *leg. III Gallicae, item* › *leg. VI Ferratae item* › *leg. II Adiutricis, item* › *leg. V Mac. item p.p. eiusdem* · · · · · *praeposito classis Misenatium* . . . , *praef. leg. VI. Victricis, duci legg. cohort. alarum Britannicimiarum adversus Armoricanos, proc. centenario Liburniae iure gladi, vivus ipse sibi et suis* . . . . . *est.*

D 2770

A mutilated epitaph from near Salonae in Dalmatia, most of which however can be made out:

'(*Dis Manibus*). *Lucius Artorius Castus, Centurion in Legion III Gallica, Centurion in Legion VI Ferrata, Centurion in Legion II Adiutrix, Centurion in Legion V Macedonica, Senior Centurion of the same Legion,* · · · · · · · · · · *Commandant of the Fleet at Misenum,* · · · · · · · · · · *Quartermaster of Legion VI Victrix, Commander of the Legionaries, (Auxiliary) Cohorts, and Cavalry Regiments of the Britannicimian* (sic) *Army against the Armoricans, Governor of Liburnia with Power of Capital Punishment, in his own lifetime* [*erected this tomb*] *for himself and his, and* [*is buried here* (?)]'

p.p. = *primus pilus*, cf. No. 16, etc.

A *procurator centenarius* was a second-grade procurator, receiving a salary of 100,000 sesterces, about £800 in gold, per annum.

THE REUNITED EMPIRE

A few milestones and altars commemorate Aurelian and his successors; for instance, one, now lost, of a group of milestones from Bitterne, near Southampton, the Roman port of Clausentum:

213)   IMP CAES LV
                 C I O   D O M I
                 TIO AVRELIANO

2272

'*For the Emperor Caesar Lucius Domitius Aurelianus.*'

A milestone from somewhere on Hadrian's Wall and a recently discovered altar from Birdoswald date from the time of M. Aurelius Probus (276-82), one of the greatest of the Illyrian soldier-emperors:

214)   M   A   V   R   215)   I   O   M
           P   R   O   B   V   S   COH · I · AEL
           PF   INVIC   D A C O R VM
           AVG   P R O B I ANA
                                             C   P   AVR
2300   V E R I N V S
                                                   T R I B

'*Marcus Aurelius Probus pius
felix invictus Augustus.*'   *J.R.S.* LI (1961), p. 194.

(215) '*To Jupiter Best and Greatest, the 1st Hadrian's Dacian Cohort,
Emperor Probus' Own, under Aurelius Verinus, Tribune.*'

   C P = *cui praeest.*

But within a few more years a new defence-problem had given
rise to a new usurpation.

THE SAXON SHORE

Since the earliest days of the occupation the *Classis Britannica*, in
addition to acting as a transport command for the army, had
patrolled the coasts and protected shipping, not least in the
Straits of Dover. Its headquarters appear to have been at Boulogne
(Bononia), and in Britain the epigraphic record is meagre, being
confined to a few tiles with the stamp,

216) CLASIS BRIT (*sic*) or, more frequently, CL BR,
RIB II

and one small altar, dedicated at Lympne (Portus Lemanis) in the
time of Hadrian:

217)   N] E P T V N [O
                           A R A M
                         L · AVFIDIVS
                         P A N T E R A
                         P R A E F E C T
                         CLAS · BRIT
66

'*To Neptune, (this) altar (is dedicated by) Lucius Aufidius Pantera,
Commander of the British Fleet.*'

   Aufidius Panthera (elsewhere so spelt), in the course of a

regular equestrian career, had commanded cavalry under Hadrian on the Danube, where he figures in a diploma. Maenius Agrippa, (Nos. 88, 89, above) may have been his successor in this naval command.

But quite early in the third century, a sign that all is not entirely well on the Kentish coast comes when soldiers also have to be stationed there, and a large fort (eight acres) is built or restored to accommodate a cohort as well as other (naval ?) personnel. Fragments of a building-inscription recently discovered at Regulbium (Reculver) read:

218)

$$A E D E M P [r i n c i p] IORVM$$
$$C V [m \cdot b] A S I L I C A \cdot$$
$$S V [b \cdot \cdot R \cdot \cdot I O RVFINO$$
$$C [o] S$$
$$\cdots \cdots F O r] T V N A T V S$$
$$\cdots \cdots r e s t i t u i] T$$

(or *a solo aedificavit ?*)

Richmond in *Antiquaries' Journal*, 1961; Wright in *JRS* LI (1961); R. P. Harper in *Anatolian Studies*, XIV (1964), p. 164

The ends of lines 1 and 3 are shortened by means of small letters and ligaturing.

'This headquarters building with its colonnade (or *"cross-hall"*) *was built* (or *restored*) *by . . . Fortunatus, under .r..ius Rufinus, consular Governor,'*

—— sc. Governor of Upper Britain under Severus' division of the province. (Lower Britain was praetorian.) The emperor's name is absent, though we have part of the top of the stone; it must have been on a separate slab. For the governor's name we seem to need, to fill the gaps, which are measurable, a name with one letter before the R, of which the lower part is preserved, and two letters between R and IVS. The 'bill' would be filled by Q. Aradius Rufinus, of a well-known senatorial family from Asia-Minor, assuming that his first initial was omitted as often at this time. He was consul about or after 220, and would be due for a consular command soon after that. Aulus Triarius Rufinus, cos. 210, would be possible, but would crowd the space a little uncomfortably.

The Cohort was the 1st Baetasian, Roman Citizens, named here in the *Notitia*, confirmed by a solitary tile, stamped COH I B. Such extreme abbreviations are quite common when there is no other regiment with the same initial in the vicinity. It is a regiment which figures in the great Brigetio Diploma of 122 (then not yet 'C.R.'); emphasises this distinction (newly won ?) in an inscription from Scotland (*RIB* 2170), and had since then had experience in the coastal fort at Alauna near Maryport in Cumberland (*RIB* 837-8, 842-3).

The trouble was with the piratical raids of the Saxons, a new enemy, from the coast of Frisia. Despite all efforts it grew through the century, and the command on the Saxon Shore, as the Channel coasts came to be called, became an important one. This is the background to the well-known adventure of Carausius.

Carausius

About 287, Carausius, a Menapian from the Belgian coast, commander (whether or not yet called Count) of the Saxon Shore, heard that he was being accused of letting raiders get through, in order to relieve them of their booty on the way back, to his own no small advantage. It may have been true; or it may have been impossible to do much better. But he was popular enough in Britain to be able, when threatened with 'liquidation', to proclaim himself emperor here and on the Gallic coast, and, behind his 'wooden walls' to defy Maximian, Emperor in the west as colleague of Diocletian.

The chief surviving documents of Carausius are the legends on his coins, and these yield a considerable amount of information. They are propaganda, but both they and the number and composition of the coins give a good impression not only of his aims but of his achievement.

219) Coins of Carausius

(*a*) With type showing Britannia greeting her deliverer: EXPECTATE VENI.—'*Come, O long looked for!*'

(*b*) With type showing heads of Diocletian, Maximian and Carausius. Obverse: CARAVSIVS ET FRATRES SVI.—'*Carausius and his Brethren.*' Reverse: PAX AVGGG.—'*The Peace of the Three Emperors.*'

(*c*) VICTORIA GERMANICA.—'*Victory over the Germans.*'

(*d*) VBERITAS AVG.—'*Prosperity under our Emperor.*'
(*e*) FELICITAS TEMPORVM.—'*Happiness of our Times.*'
(*f*) RESTITVTOR SAECVLI.—'*Restorer of the Age.*'
(*g*) RENOVATIO ROMANORVM.—'*Renewal of the Roman race.*'
(*h*) ROMA AETERNA.—'*Rome, Eternal.*'

Among the gods represented on his coins appear Jupiter Optimus Maximus, Mars, Neptune, Oceanus and, Hercules Pacifer—the subduer of the forces of disorder and lawless power. Such legends as (*d*) and (*e*) show that Carausius aimed at and boasted of the restoration or maintenance of economic prosperity; and the fact that his coins, unlike those of his contemporaries on the continent, are of good silver, shows that the boast was well grounded. (*b*) shows him trying to come to terms with Diocletian and Maximian; but their mints issued no responsive civilities. (*g*) and (*h*) show the emphasis that he laid on his position as a Roman Caesar Augustus; and (*c*) assures us that he carried out the task for which he was first appointed admiral by defeating the Saxons—how seriously, we do not know. (*a*), finally even contains an echo of Vergil (*Aen*. II, 283).

But the career of this able usurper was cut short after seven years by a conspiracy among his officers, one of whom, by name Allectus, murdered and succeeded him.

220)   A COIN OF ALLECTUS

Obverse: ALLECTVS ET FRATRES SVI.
Reverse: PAX AVGGG.

The coin is a close copy of 219(*b*) above, and shows that Allectus too tried to gain recognition by the Augusti. He seems, however, to have lacked the ability and failed to win the popularity of Carausius; and already the new Caesar in command in the west, Constantius, surnamed Chlorus, had recaptured his continental foothold at Boulogne. Then, in 296, Constantius and his Praetorian Prefect Asclepiodotus crossed the Channel, in two separate squadrons, under cover of fog. Constantius and his fleet lost their way, but Asclepiodotus made good his landing on the south coast and marched on London. Allectus hastened to intercept him, but was defeated and killed. His Frankish mercenaries, decimated in the battle and with their master dead, fled

CONSTANTIUS ENTERS LONDON

By kind permission of the Trustees of the British Museum

Plate 6

for home; and before taking ship from London, they were just beginning to loot the city, when the missing squadron under Constantius, arriving just in time, dropped anchor in London River, and his soldiers cut down the demoralised plunderers in the streets.

CONSTANTIUS IN LONDON

Once more our only contemporary written document is a coin— a splendid gold medallion, found near Arras in 1922. On the obverse it bears the head of Constantius. On the reverse, the conqueror, lance in hand, rides over a bridge to the gate of a walled town, before which a kneeling figure, representing London, welcomes her deliverer with outstretched hands. In the foreground is the river, where there rides a Roman galley crowded with armed men. The legends are:

221) Obverse: FL VAL CONSTANTIVS NOBIL CAES.

    Reverse: REDDITOR LVCIS AETERNAE, and, beneath the kneeling female figure, the syllable: LON   (Plate 6).

'*Flavius Valerius Constantius, the Noble Caesar, Restorer of Light Eternal. London.*'

THE END OF THE ADVENTURE: A MILESTONE

The whole episode is summarised in the two inscriptions on a milestone found near Carlisle. One is the only extant stone inscription of Carausius:

222) (*a*)

	IMP	C	M
	AVR	MAVS	
	CARAVSIO P F		
2291	INVICTO AVG		

'*In honour of the Emperor, Caesar, Marcus Aurelius Mausaeus Carausius the Good, the Fortunate, the Unconquered, Augustus.*'

Here as on his coins, Carausius emphasises the continuity of his government with that of the great days of the Empire, using, like Victorinus (No. 209) the old style '*Imperator Caesar*', rather than '*Dominus Noster*', and assuming the time-honoured names of Marcus Aurelius, as well as the now stereotyped titles *Pius* and *Felix*.

R B.——M

(*b*)   On the same stone, opposite end, opposite way up:

FL VAL
C O N S
T A N T [I
N O N O B
C A E S

2292

'*To Flavius Valerius Constantinus, the Noble Caesar.*'

This is Constantine the Great, son of Constantius, as Caesar in Britain in 306-7.

CONSTANTIUS AND THE NORTHERN FRONTIER

But if, as his milestone suggests, Carausius had maintained order in the north, in the last few years things had not gone well there. A unique inscription found by E. B. Birley at Birdoswald in 1929 suggests that Constantius, like Severus after Albinus' usurpation, had to set on foot extensive repairing and rebuilding; though, characteristically of the age, we have only this, and one fragment, to set beside the dozens of Severan stones. When Constantius' troops approached the great fort of Camboglanna they found it waste and ruinous, with grass growing in the chinks of the deserted walls. The inscription, it is true, merely tells us that the place had 'fallen into decay' (cf. No. 195); but Roman military buildings did not usually spontaneously fall to pieces in a matter of eighty years.

223)   DD]NN   ·   DIOC[LETIANO]   ·   ET
M[AXIM]IANO INVICTIS AVGG · ET
CONSTANTIO   ET   ·   MAXIMIANO
NN · CC · SVB · VP · AVR · ARPAGIO PR
PRAETOR · QUOD ERAT HVMO COPERT
ET IN LABE CONL·ET PRINC·ET BAL·REST
CVRANT · FL · MARTINO CENT · PP · C·····

1912

'*For our Lords Diocletian and Maximian the Invincible Augusti, and Constantius and Maximian the Noble Caesars, under His Excellency Aurelius Arpagius the Governor, the Praetorium, which was overgrown and fallen into decay, and the Headquarters and Bath-House [or: Catapult-*

emplacements] *were restored, under the superintendence of Flavius Martinus, Centurion, commanding the* · · · · · *Cohort.'*

Of the abbreviations, DDNN = *dominis nostris*; NN · CC = *nobilissimis Caesaribus*; VP = *viro perfectissimo*; PR = *praeses*, or rather *praeside*; and PRAETOR, here, is short for *praetorium*. The next clause, in full, runs *quod erat humo copertum et in labe conlapsum, et principia et balneum*—the bath-house adjoining the fort—or, as Birley prefers, *ballistaria*, the catapult-emplacements. REST is then either *restituta sunt*, or *restituit*, the subject in the latter case being the Cohort whose name, at the very end of the inscription, has been lost. CENT may be either *Centurione* or, as the abbreviation for 'Centurion' is usually shorter—C, Ɔ, or ›—perhaps (*procuratore*) *centenario*, 'second-grade procurator' (cf. No. 212). PP = *praepositus*, and C is the beginning of the lost title of the Cohort.

This inscription settled one hitherto open question about the terminology of a Roman camp or fort—the question whether the *principia*, the headquarters buildings, were or were not the same as, or including, the *praetorium*. From this stone it is clear that the two are separate and distinct; the *praetorium* will be simply the commandant's house.

It is also worth noting that His Perfection—to use the official language of the time—Aurelius Arpagius, the governor, bears a barbarian name.

§3   CONSTANTINE AND CHRISTIANITY

CONSTANTINE THE GREAT: A MILESTONE

224)

IMP CAES
FLAV VAL
CONSTANTINO
PIO NOB
CAES
DIVI
C]ONSTANTI
PII
AVG
FILIO

2233

'To the Emperor Flavius Valerius Constantinus the Good, the Noble Caesar, Son of the late Deified Emperor Constantius the Good, Augustus.'

This stone is of interest not only as one of the dozen in Britain (all milestones) naming the Emperor who made Christianity the state religion, but also because it comes from Cornwall. Roman remains are rare west of Exeter; but in the third century the tin mines, which had gone out of production, perhaps because of Spanish competition, began again to be worked. Five milestones, dating from Gordian to Constantine, remain as the only imperial Roman inscriptions in the county.

The mention of Constantine's father on three milestones, though not unparalleled, suggests continuing veneration for the memory of Constantius in Britain.

CHRISTIANITY

Before the end of his reign, Diocletian 'called off' his persecution of Christianity. By the famous proclamation of Constantine, Christianity became the religion of the State. By the end of the fourth century, other cults were proscribed. In short, Christianity was the dominant religion of the Empire during the last hundred years of Roman government in Britain; and yet traces of it among Romano-British remains are few. This has often caused surprise; but it would cease to do so if it were realised how very few Roman inscriptions of any kind remain from Britain in this period. If fourth-century had been one-quarter as common as second-century or Severan inscriptions, Christianity would have left its mark. Very likely it was late in making progress in this remote and thinly populated province; but the Church in Britain was vigorous enough to have produced its protomartyr, the soldier Albanus, St. Alban, some time in the third century, and the arch-heretic Pelagius, who had a great following in the island, at the end of the fourth. His heresy, by the way, consisted in rejecting the doctrine of man's total depravity. If I *ought* to do something, he argues, it follows that I *can*. 'What is unavoidable is not sin; and what depends on our wills *can* be avoided.' He therefore rejected Augustine's view that man's only hope of escaping damnation lay in divine grace, mediated through the Church. His view had political overtones; for *gratia* in his world also meant the often corrupt 'grace and favour' of organs of the government, whereas he stood for self-help. If there are any persons who still think in terms of 'Celtic' or 'Latin' or 'Teutonic' psychology, it is interesting to note that this Briton produced a very *English* heresy!

A Tombstone

225)

	D			M	
FLAS	ANTIGONS	P A P I A S			
C I V I S	GRECVS	VIXIT	ANNOS		
P L V S	MINVS	LX	QVEM	AD	
M O D V M	A C C O M O D A T A M				
FATIS	ANIMAM	REVOCAVIT			
SEPTIMIADO · · · · · · · · · ·					

955

Carlisle. A red sandstone slab, about thirty inches by twenty, broken away at bottom. The inscription is roughly cut and obscurely worded; it may be translated:

'(To the Shades.) *Flavius Antigonus Papias, a Greek, lived sixty years more or less, at which limit he surrendered (?) his spirit resigned to its fate. Septimia Do . . . . . [his wife (?) set up this stone (?)]*'.

REVOCAVIT is given a strange meaning, and ACCOMODATAM has less than its usual allowance of m's, but that seems to be the sense. Antigonus is usually held to have been a Christian, on account of the expression 'sixty years more or less'. Pagan tombstones usually give the deceased's age in years precisely, if not accurately —sometimes in months and days too; but to the Christians it is a matter of pride not to be too much concerned about the precise length of someone's earthly life, and they frequently use the formula '*plus minus*'. D.M., 'To the Divine Shades' is a thoroughly pagan expression, but it seems to have become a mere formula, whose precise meaning was forgotten; at any rate, it occurs on several tombstones on the continent which are much more explicitly Christian than this.

The absence from this stone of any explicitly Christian words or symbols may be due to its having been set up in the third century, while the faith was still proscribed.

The Chi-Rho Monogram

However that may be, the Church has evidently triumphed by the
time of Syagrius, a fourth-century dealer in metal, who seems to
have used the ☧ monogram, the first two letters of the name of
Christ in Greek, as his trade-mark. In the Thames near Battersea
were found several ingots of tin, or rather pewter—72 to 80 per
cent tin, the rest lead—which belonged to him. They are stamped
with his name, and also with the 'Chi-Rho' and either the letters
Alpha and Omega or the Christian motto '(There is) Hope in
God'.

226)   (*a*)   SVAG
                              RIVS

                        (*b*)   SPES   IN
                                     ☧
                              DEO

                    (*c*)   A   ☧   O

BM, p. 32

Occurrences of the Chi-Rho have, indeed, been fairly numerous
among the discoveries of recent years. It appears on 'christening
spoons' in the great Mildenhall Treasure in the British Museum—
a superb silver table-service, buried in the crisis of some barbarian
invasion and never recovered; also, painted on wall plaster, in the
house-chapel of the Christian villa at Lullingstone, Kent, and in
the halo round the head (of Christ?) in the fine mosaic from the
villa at Hinton St. Mary, Dorset.

Christianity and Classical Mythology

Though frowned on by some of the Church Fathers, the classical
mythology did not die with the old religion, but lived on with the
old literature. Christians were probably all the more easily
reconciled to this, for the fact that the classical gods had for some
time past not been very real to many people. Many a Roman
gentleman in the second century must have read about Venus or
Juno in the *Aeneid* with much the same emotions, or lack of them,
as an English gentleman in the eighteenth.

Also the mythology could be allegorised. Bellerophon on his
winged steed assailing the Chimaera, for example (an allegory of a

heavenly warrior attacking evil?) seems to have been popular with Christians, and perhaps has even some connection with the ancestry of St. George and the Dragon. The scene appears both at Hinton St. Mary and Lullingstone.

Accordingly it is not very surprising to find the Christian symbol and pagan mythology combined in the decoration of another late Roman Dorsetshire manor-house.

In one of the rooms of the rich villa at Frampton, Maiden Newton, about five miles from Dorchester, was found a tessellated pavement, with mythological scenes of the usual character. One side of it was almost perfect, and showed a head of Neptune, attended by dolphins, with two lines of verse, one on each side of him. Later—when the son of the old British squire turned nominally Christian, one may imagine, and felt that it would be only decent to give his new religion at least a place, along with the old gods, in the decoration of the ancestral dining-room—a semicircular extension was added to this pavement, standing out from the middle of the side on which the head of Neptune was, and in the middle of this, surrounded by a circle, was inlaid the Chi-Rho monogram. The complete scheme of the decoration is thus as follows:

227)

(Head of Neptune)

Neptuni vertex, regmen   *Scultura cui cerulea est*
sortiti mobile venti   *delfinis cincta duobus.*

The metre of the 'poetry' bears a faint resemblance to the familiar dactylic hexameter; but it has been turned into a new and jingling 'heptameter' metre by the addition of an extra foot to each line. The Latin is queer. One may render thus:

'The head of Neptune who obtained the restless kingdom of the storm; Whose sea-blue head is in the picture encircled by two dolphins.'

THE LAST STAND OF PAGANISM

In 361-3 came the attempt of the brave and brilliant, but hopelessly romantic and conservative, Emperor Julian to restore the religion of ancient Greece. The attempt was utterly foredoomed. In a dying world, the Church was almost the only institution that showed vitality; and when the gallant Julian fell in an obscure skirmish beyond the eastern frontier, his reactionary movement collapsed at once.

While it lasted, it was probably responsible for the setting up of the last known dedicatory inscription to a Roman god by a Roman officer in Britain. It is on the damaged sandstone base of a statue of Jupiter set up at Cirencester:

228)   Face I

```
         . I . O [· M ·
         L · SEPT[IMIVS
         V·P·PR·B[RIT·PR
          RESTI[TVIT
         CIVIS · R[EMVS ?
```

II	III
SIG]NVM ET	SEPTIMIVS
E] R E C T A M	R E N O V A T
P]RISCA RE	P R I M A E
LI]GIONE CO	PROVINCIAE
L V] M N A M	RECTOR

103

Parts of (I) and (II) are broken away, but nearly all can be restored with certainty. Line 3 of the face inscription, expanded, would run *Vir perfectissimus, Praeses Britanniae Primae.* The whole, then, translates:

'*To Jupiter the Good and Great, Lucius Septimius, V.P., Governor of Britannia Prima, restored this* · · · · · .'

Britannia Prima, Britannia Secunda, Maxima Caesariensis and Flavia Caesariensis, with the later addition of Valentia (in Wales?) were the provinces into which Britain was divided after Diocletian's reorganisation. We know nothing certainly of their geography, except that Cirencester was presumably in Britannia Prima.

The second and third inscriptions are continuous, forming one sentence. They are metrical—two of the most un-Virgilian hexameters ever written, even in England. Translation:

'This statue and base, erected by ancient piety, Septimius now renews, the Governor of Britannia Prima.'

The lines scan apparently as follows:

$$\bar{S}\breve{i}gn\breve{u}m\ \breve{e}t\ |\ \bar{e}r\bar{e}ct|\bar{a}m\ \|\ \bar{p}r\bar{i}s|c\breve{a}\ r\breve{e}l\breve{i}g|\bar{i}\bar{o}n\breve{e}\ c\breve{o}l|\bar{u}mn\bar{a}m$$
$$\bar{S}\breve{e}pt\breve{i}m\breve{i}|\bar{u}s\ r\breve{e}n\breve{o}|v\bar{a}t\ \|\ pr\bar{i}m|\bar{a}e\ pr\bar{o}|v\breve{i}nc\breve{i}ae\ |\ r\bar{e}ct\breve{o}r.$$

Final -um before a vowel is not elided, and in the scansions religione and *provinciae* the classical scansion by quantity seems to be giving way to scansion by stress-accent, as in mediaeval Latin.

§4   TWILIGHT

For the last fifty years of the Roman occupation, scarcely an inscription remains, unless coins be included. Coins do in fact give some information. Numerous hoards have been found, including coins of various dates down to about the middle of the fourth century, but none later; hoards, therefore, which were buried about 350 or soon after. The prosperity which Britain had so long enjoyed, while the continental provinces were crossed and recrossed by hostile armies, is coming to an end. When so many people bury their money, there is a feeling of insecurity in the air; and when so many people die without returning to reclaim it, we may be sure that the threatening blow has fallen.

We are thrown back upon the literary sources, represented, for once, by a really good historian, Ammianus Marcellinus. As usual, literary history gives us no such material for reconstructing the everyday life of an age as the inscriptions give us for the second century. Ammianus does, however, give the bare facts concerning the most terrible blow that had ever befallen Roman Britain.

In 364, he says, it seemed as though some hostile god had sounded a trumpet giving the signal for assault to the enemies of Rome. The barbarians poured in on every frontier; on every frontier the local armies must stand and fight, without hope of reinforcements from other provinces, themselves no less hard pressed. In Britain there was war against Saxon and Frankish raiders on the east and south coasts, against the Scots invading from Ireland, against the 'painted men' in the north. It went on for three years, with continual harassing warfare and continued wastage of men. Then suddenly the breaking-point was reached. Nectaridus, Count of the Saxon Shore, was killed in battle; Fullofaudes the Dux Britanniarum, 'Duke of the Britains', fell into an ambuscade. The defence collapsed, and Britain paid the penalty, as Roman provinces so often did, for an imperial system that divided the Empire into hard shell and soft pulp—professional soldiers on the frontier and a civilian populace, *forbidden by law to bear arms*, behind. The barbarians overran the country, moving all the faster for the network of Roman roads, though it is unlikely that they took any of the larger walled towns. Plunderers appeared even in the south-east around London. Fortunately, help was at hand. The desperate messengers who sped to the Emperor Valentinian I found him beginning to make head against the enemy on the German frontier, and in 368 his general Theodosius landed with an army in Kent and took charge of the defence.

He met with less resistance than might have been expected. Many raiders no doubt retired with their booty, and a Roman field-army in battle array was still invincible. But he had to reorganise the demoralised British forces before he could conduct his great sweeping movement across the country; it must have been both a brilliant and a laborious campaign that ended in 369 with the re-establishment of the northern frontier on the line of Hadrian's Wall.

This time the Wall yields not even a single inscription to confirm the inference of a reoccupation, based by archaeologists on coin-finds and the existence of a fourth level, at Birdoswald, for instance, in which inscriptions both of Severus and Constantius served for flooring.

That, however, is the story of those hoards of coins, buried and never retrieved. This was the disaster in which most of the prosperous Romano-British manor-houses went up in flames. It was a blow from which Roman Britain never recovered. Whether she could have recovered we cannot know; that she was never given the chance was due to the ambitions of yet another imperial general.

MAXIMUS

Magnus Maximus, a Spaniard, had held a high command under Theodosius in 368-9. Many years later he was still—or again—in Britain; in Wales, which was being threatened by Irish raiders, the Scoti. In 383 he caused his troops to proclaim him emperor, crossed to the continent, defeated and killed the Emperor Gratian and since, of the other Augusti, Valentinian II was a boy and Theodosius (son of Maximus' old general) was facing Goths in the Balkans, was able to secure an agreement by which he was recognised as Augustus, ruling over Britain, Gaul and Spain.

Several inscriptions, though none found in Britain, show us Maximus thus officially recognised; for instance, this extract from a vote of thanks for services rendered, passed by a local Senate in honour of a citizen of Africa Tripolitana:

229) - - *Salvis ac toto orbe vincentibus dddd. nnnn. FFFFllll. Valentiniano Theodosio Arcadio et Maximo semper August - - -*

D 787. Gigthis, Tripolitania.

'*During the reign and victorious supremacy throughout the whole world of our lords the Four Flavii, Valentinian, Theodosius, Arcadius and Maximus the ever-ruling Augusti - -*'

Maximus' name has been defaced later, like that of Albinus under similar circumstances (No. 192).

Flavius, a family name of the house of Constantine (cf. No. 224, etc.) has acquired the same sort of prestige as the name of Aurelius in an earlier century, and passes to later emperors by a similar process of fictitious adoption.

Valentinian was the son of Valentinian I, and brother of Gratian; Arcadius, Theodosius' elder son.

MAXIMUS IN ITALY: A MILESTONE

230) *DD. nn. Magno Maximo et Fl. Victori invictis et perpetuis Augustis, b. r. p. n. IIIIII*

D 788. From near Brescia. Several similar stones have been found both in north and central and south Italy.

'*To our Lords Magnus Maximus and Flavius Victor, the invincible and evre-ruling Augusti, born for the well-being of the State. (To Brescia,) (Six Miles).*'

b. r. p. n. = bono rei publicae natis, a current formula.

In 387 Maximus broke the treaty, crossed the Alps and seized Italy. This stone shows him momentarily supreme there. He has broken with his late colleagues and associated with himself as Emperor Flavius Victor, his young son; and local authorities hasten to put up the usual loyal dedications. The rule in Italy of this 'Eternal Augustus' actually lasted about one year. Theodosius decided that the time had come to make an end of him. Maximus, after two defeats in what is now Jugoslavia, was taken prisoner and put to death at Aquileia.

Maximus' career was a disaster, squandering the forces of the hard-pressed empire; but his was probably a magnetic character. His name was remembered in Britain. As Maxen Wledig, Lord Maximus, he figures among Roman Emperors at the head of the genealogies of later Welsh princes, and a romance of his conquest of Rome, *The Dream of Macsen Wledig*, is among the Welsh stories called the *Mabinogion*.

Maximus also, when in Gaul in 385, has the invidious distinction of having been, at the behest of the local bishops, the first Christian ruler to execute heretics, the followers of Priscillian of Spain. St. Martin of Tours, hermit and bishop, who had started his career as a cavalry officer, raised his voice in lone protest at this use of the secular arm. A strong 'wind of change' towards the Middle Ages is blowing here.

The Last Roman Inscriptions of Britain

In 395 and after, for the last time a great Roman general campaigned in Britain: Stilicho the Vandal, chief marshal of Honorius, the younger son of Theodosius, who reigned over the west, but did not govern, from the marsh-protected fortress of Ravenna. Arcadius, his elder brother, ruled in Constantinople. Their coins are the last imperial issues to reach Britain. Honorius is also represented by stamped tiles recording work (Stilicho's?) at the Saxon Shore fort of Anderida (Pevensey):

231)   HON AVG ANDRIA
RIB II

Honorius Augustus: Anderida.

Stilicho probably also reorganised the signal-towers on high points of the Yorkshire coast, which now gave early warning of the approach of Saxons or sea-borne Picts ('Painted Men': late Roman Britain's abusive name for the Caledonian tribes). And from one of these, at Ravenscar, north of Scarborough, comes, rough and illiterate, the last stone inscription naming Roman officers:

232)
                        IVSTINIANVSPP
                        VINDICIANVS
                        MASBIERIVRR
                        MCASTRVMEECIT
                        ASO
721

The gibberish of the third line and the better effort of the fourth and fifth have been interpreted as an illiterate stone-cutter's misreading of his copy (which would be easy, from late Roman cursive) for *magister* (a late Roman military rank) *turrem* (et) *castrum fecit a so*(lo). So:

'*Justinianus, officer commanding* (praepositus). *Vindicianus,* magister built (this) tower (and) fort from the ground up.'

This Justinianus might be identical—though with difficulty, if the inscription dates from a first foundation of the fort by Theodosius, about 370—with a later general, who briefly appears in the Greek history of Zosimus, as an officer of the last British usurping emperor.

Exactly at the turn of the year, 406-7, the Rhine frontier finally collapsed, when a horde of Germans crossed the frozen river near Mainz. Britain, left isolated, again produced its own emperors: a soldier, Marcus, then a civilian, Gratian, both soon murdered, and finally another soldier, Constantine, trading on his name. He crossed to Gaul and gained recognition from Honorius, who from fear of Stilicho had murdered him, and was now in straits, with Alaric at the gates of Rome. But he failed to round up the barbarian invaders; one of his own generals, Gerontius (Geraint), rose against him, and he was finally captured and executed by Honorius' general and brother-in-law, Constantius. It was now that Honorius wrote to Britain, denuded of regular forces, that the *civitates* there must defend themselves.

Post-Roman Inscriptions

The last control of Britain from Rome may thus be said to end, with great precision, on New Year's Day, 407, shortly after midnight. This is not the place in which to speak of the not unsuccessful efforts to defend themselves which the Britons did make. But a few sub-Roman inscriptions do illustrate both the continued danger of raids from overseas, and the re-emergence of a sub-Roman Celtic, largely Christian, semi-civilisation.

Loot in Ireland

Stamp on a silver ingot, found along with nearly 1500 Roman coins of the late fourth century, near Coleraine in County Derry:

233)   EXOFPA
                         TRICI

BM, pp. 72f

'*From the workshop of Patricius.*'

OF stands for *officina*.

The coins date the hoard to a time when Britain was constantly being raided by the Scots from Ireland; it is someone's share of the loot. The name of the legal owner, Patricius, is, as the *British Museum Guide* remarks, an interesting coincidence; for about the same time another Patricius was carried off by Irish raiders, as a boy, from Britain. He was afterwards known as St. Patrick.

Some Celtic Tombstones

Actually, one sequel of the end of Roman government is a slight *increase* in the number of inscriptions, though they are only tombstones of the roughest kind. Chiefs, at least for the most part—not ordinary people—now living a Homeric and dangerous life with no one over them but God, had enough pride to wish their names to be commemorated on their *tumuli*. The typical sub-Roman inscribed stone is a pillar, like one of the roughest Roman milestones, with the name of the deceased, usually in the genitive, and sometimes his father's. Often there is a companion inscription in Ogham, the Irish alphabet in which the Latin letters are represented by combinations of short and long strokes on one or both sides of a centre line; an arrangement apparently adapted for cutting with a knife on the corner of a squared timber post. Sometimes the oghams seem to have been intentionally defaced later—perhaps by Christians who associated the Irish signs with paganism. R. A. S. Macalister in his *Corpus Inscr. Insularum Celticarum* collects 149 early post-Roman inscriptions from Wales, 31 from Cornwall, 11 from adjacent counties of England and 15, of very various dates and characters, from Scotland. One of the earliest is an outlier, and in oghams alone. It was set up in Silchester (Calleva of the Atrebates) evidently already ruinous but still inhabited (*CIIC* I, No. 496): the Irish name Ebicatos Maqi (Mac, son of) —— and clan, represented by 'Muco ——'; the details of his ancestry seem to have been defaced even before the stone, which 'looks like the finial of a large balustrade' (Macalister) was pushed into a well, itself dug through the floors of a Romano-British house. What was this Irishman doing there? Was he a mercenary, fighting the Saxons? In any case, the stone and its fate give a glimpse of slum conditions in Silchester, between the breakdown of civilisation in the south-east and the definitive English occupation.

A sub-Roman stone from Chesterholm on Hadrian's Wall (cf. Nos 172ff.) this time in Latin letters only, attests some continuation of life at that fort and village:

234)   BRIGOMAGLOS - - -
CIIC I, 498

There are traces of some more letters, which have been very variously read.

On Winsford Hill, Somerset, a pillar reads in Latin only, vertically downwards:

235)   ]s
                        CARAĀCI
                        NEPVS
CIIC I, 499

The name in the first line has been chipped away, Macalister thought 'apparently with intention'. Rhys, followed in the first edition of this book, interpreted the rest as 'clan of Caratacus'; but Macalister reads the name as Caranacus, insisting that the line over the second A signifies N and is not a ligatured T, and would render *nepus* as Latin *nepos*, grandson.

Not surprisingly, some of the most literate inscriptions are the work of churchmen. Five in Wigtonshire, the south-west corner of Scotland, are commonly associated with the Whithorn mission of St. Ninian, himself a Romano-British citizen, whose mission was launched just before the final severance of communication with the Roman government. Early date is suggested both by letter-forms and by the form of the cross with which three of them, at Kirkmadrine near Stranraer, are decorated: with the curved member of a Greek Rho springing from the top of each, so as to make the early, Constantinian form of the XP or Chi-Rho sign. The finest and clearest of the Kirkmadrine stones reads:

236)   A   ET   [O

                              HIC IACENT
                              SCI ET PRAE
                              CIPVISACER
                              DOTES IDEST
                              V I V ENTIVS
                              ETMAVORIVS

CIIC I, 516   Plate 7

'*Hic iacent sancti et praecipui sacerdotes, id est Viventius et Mavorius.*'

The T of *id est* is damaged, but not sufficiently to constitute an excuse for reading *Ides* as a third (and singularly unconvincing) proper name! So:

'(*Alpha and Omega.* XP.) *Here lie holy and notable priests, that is, Viventius and Mavorius.*'

Historically, one of the most interesting is a royal tombstone from Caermarthen; a large rough stone eighty inches in height by forty-two across, inscribed in Ogham and Latin.

237)   MEMORIA
                         V O T E P O R I G I S
                         P R O T I C T O R I S

CIIC, I, 358

'*Monument of Voteporix the Protector.*'

THE CHURCH SURVIVES

Reproduced by kind permission of the Society of Antiquaries of Scotland

Plate 7

This meaning of *memoria* is regular in early Christian Latin.

The oghams read 'Votecorigas'—the same name, with the substitution of a guttural, as in the Goidelic Celtic languages, where Welsh has the labial P. This is almost certainly Vorteporius, King of the Demetae of South Wales, criticised in the lamentations 'On the Destruction of Britain' of the sixth-century writer Gildas. The same name appears in the form Guortepir in a Welsh pedigree, earlier in which appear the names Protec and Protector.

This, then, is a true relic of the Celtic revival, the tombstone of one of those Welsh kings who lived in the Indian summer of Gildas' own day, after the mutiny of the German 'federates' (the English) had been temporarily broken at the Siege of Mons Badonicus.

A PRINCE OF CORNWALL

Another 'long stone', 8½ feet high, from Castle Dore on the hills above Fowey harbour, bears an inscription similarly reading vertically downwards. It is weathered and in parts almost illegible, but has been much studied. It now stands at the Fowey-Lostwithiel-Bodinnick crossroads. Castle Dore is an early iron-age fortress, reoccupied in the sub-Roman period. Dr Ralegh Radford has discovered in it sixth-century red 'samian' pottery which must have been imported from the Mediterranean.

238)   CIRVSINIVSHICIACIT
                         CVNOWORIFILIVS

CIIC I, 487

'*Here lies Cirusinius, son of Cunomorus.*'

Iacit for *iacet* and the inverted M in form of a W are both quite familiar phenomena in this age.

Cunomorus ('Seal'?), who set up, or whose family set up, this large and conspicuous monument, was evidently an important person. Do we know any more about him? We do. The *Life* of an early sixth-century Cornish saint, Paulus Aurelianus, who migrated to Brittany like thousands of other Britons of his time, recounts that he was for a short time persuaded to leave his monastic retirement by 'King Marcus Quonomorus' (a misguided attempt to improve the spelling, by a ninth-century editor of the *Life*), to act as Bishop of his kingdom. This king, bearing a

R.B.—N

Latin as well as a British name, is famous under the former: he is King Mark of Cornwall, of the Arthurian cycle of romance.

Who, then, was the deceased? I have faithfully followed Macalister's reading. But, as he notes, Rhys read the name as DRVSTAGNI. The first I is at least very close to the C; an inverted D, 'ɑ', is not unknown in British inscriptions even of the Roman empire; and the last letters of the name are very faint indeed. Ralegh Radford in the *Journal of the Royal Institution of Cornwall* for 1951 (pp. 117-19), argues for a return to the name DRVSTAGNVS, and is followed by Mr John Morris, who in his article on Celtic Saints in *Past and Present*, no. 11 (1957), note 13, draws attention also to the evidence from the *Life of Paul Aurelian*. (See also his history of Britain *c.* 350-650, *The Age of Arthur*, forthcoming.) In his belief, this is the name of Drostan or Tristan, who in the romances is King Mark's nephew. If his tragic love was actually for *his father's* young bride, whom he was bringing home from Ireland—the Phaedra-Hippolytus situation—it is intelligible that the romancers might have made the relationship less close, in order to be able to keep Tristan as a hero without offending the Church.

A SAXON GRAVE

Our last inscription is not Latin but Greek; it is on a greenish glass cup, a precious possession at that time:

239)   ουγιενων χρω
BM

'*Good health to the user*'—corresponding to the Latin *utere felix* of No. 134. It is in vernacular Greek; ουγιενων shows us the current pronunciation of classical *ὑγιαίνων*. The cup must have come originally—by what vicissitudes?—from the still civilised Byzantine east; and it gains significance from the situation in which it was found, in the grave of a chieftain of the Saxon invaders, on High Down, near Brighton.

> 'To-day the Roman and his trouble
> Are ashes under Uricon.'

But Latin was never extinct in the Celtic west even in the fifth and sixth centuries.

NOTE ON BOOKS

The availability of printed texts of inscriptions has enormously increased since the first edition of this book appeared in 1932.

Collingwood and Wright, *The Roman Inscriptions of Britain*, Vol. I (O.U.P., 1965; £12 12s), contains all those on stone and some on other materials discovered up to the end of 1954. Vol. II, containing those on pottery, metal, etc., is in preparation; and a supplement to Vol. I containing more recent discoveries will no doubt appear in due course. Vol. I should be found in all major libraries.

Several books dealing with parts of the subject of Roman Britain publish all the inscriptions relevant to their themes; e.g.:

Sir George Macdonald, *The Roman Wall in Scotland* (1911; in libraries).

V. E. Nash-Williams, *The Roman Frontier in Wales* (Cardiff: University of Wales, 1954; 30s).

P. Salway, *The Frontier People of Roman Britain* (C.U.P., 1965; £3), with 112 inscrs. recording civilians in the northern area.

G. Webster and D. R. Dudley, *The Roman Conquest of Britain* (to A.D. 60; Batsford, 1965; 30s); nine inscrs.

For those from outside Britain, reference may still be made to the *Corpus*, with more recent supplements to some volumes; especially, for Britain and the Army, to Vol. XVI, ed. H. Nesselhauf, with its two supplements, containing all the known military diplomas, with discussions and indexes; also to *Inscriptiones Latinae Selectae* (H. Dessau). These expensive publications will rarely be found outside the chief academic or reference libraries. The Cambridge University Press has, however, produced some useful volumes of *Documents* (including also papyri), including: M. P. Charlesworth, *Documents Illustrating the Reigns of Claudius and Nero* (1st edn. 1939).

M. McCrum and A. G. Woodhead, *Select Documents of the Principates of the Flavian Emperors* (1961; 27s 6d).

E. M. Smallwood, *Documents Illustrating the Principates of Nerva, Trajan and Hadrian* (1966; 42s).

Only the last of these contains an index. Volumes on the

Antonines and the Severi will be a welcome addition to the series.

For the publication of new discoveries in Britain, see R. P. Wright in the *Journal of Roman Studies*, annually; and for the whole Roman world, the Paris *Année épigraphique*.

Lastly, for the results obtained from epigraphy in this field, reference may be made, as in the text, to Professor Birley's collection of articles, *Roman Britain and the Roman Army* (Kendal: T. Wilson, 1953; 15s); and to the new large history of ancient Britain, Sheppard Frere's *Britannia* (Routledge & Kegan Paul, 1967; £4 4s).

GLOSSARY
of Abbreviations used in Roman Inscriptions

These abbreviations are extremely numerous. Appended are some of the commoner and less obvious, most of which occur in this book. There is a longer list in Collingwood, *Archaeology of Roman Britain.*

A	Adiutrix, animo, Aulus, Aurelius	FAB	Fabius (—a), fabri
AD(I)	Adiutrix, Adiabenicus	FAL	Falerna
AEM	Aemilius, (—a)	F.C	faciendum curavit
AN	annus	FL(A)	Flavius
ANI	Aniensis	G	Gaius, genius
ARN	Arnensis	GAL	Galeria, Gallica, —oram
AVR	Aurelius (—a)	GEM	Gemina
BEN. B.F.,	beneficiarius	GER	Germanus (—icus)
B.M.	bene merens	GN	Gnaeus
BR	Britannia, Brittones, Breuci, Bracaraugustani	HAS	Hastatus
		HOR	Horatia
B.R.P.N	Bono rei publicae natus	H.F.C	Heres faciendum curavit
C	Caesar, Gaius, civis, cohors, coniux, cuius, curavit	H.S.E	Hic situs est
		I.O.M	Jovi Optimo Maximo
		K	Kalendae
C.A	curam agit (—ens)	L	Lucius, locus
CAM	Camilia	LEG	Legatus, legio
CHO	cohors	LEM	Lemonia
CL(A)	Classis, Claudius (—a)	LIB	libertus
CLV	Clustumina	M	Marcus, miles, militavit, mille milliaria
COL	collegium, Collina		
COR	Cornelia, cornicularius, corona	M'	Manius
		MAEC	Maecia
COS	Consul (—es, —aris)	MEN	Menenia
C.P	cui praeest	M.F.P.	Mater filio posuit
C.R	Civis Romanus	N	noster, numen, numerus, nummus
D	dat, Decimus, decretum, designatus, deus, divus, Dolichenus, dominus, Domitius, domo, donat, donum		
		NNCC	Nobilissimi Caesares
		OF	officina, Oufentina
		ORD	Ordinarius
		OVF	Oufentina
D.D	decreto decurionum	P	passus, pedes, Pius, Publius posuit, potestas
DDNN	Domini nostri		
D.M.(S)	Dis Manibus (Sacrum)	PAL	Palatina
D.N	Dominus noster	PAP	Papiria
D.S.D	de suo dedit	PED	pedes, pedites
D.S.P	de sua pecunia, de suo posuit	P.F	Pater fecit, Pia Fidelis, Pius Felix
EQ	eques, equitata		
ER	heres	P.M	Pontifex maximus
ESQ	Esquilina	PO(P)	Publilia
F	fecit, felix, fidelis, filius	POL	Pollia

POM	Pomptina	TI	Tiberius
P.P	Pater Patriae, pagus posuit	TR	Tribunus (—icia)
P.R	Populus Romanus	TRO	Tromentina
PR	Praefectus, praeses, praetor (—ius), princeps, provincia	V	Valeria, victrix, vir, vivus, vixit, votum
PROC	Proconsul, procurator	VAL	Valerius (—a)
PR.PR.	Praefectus praetorio, pro praetore	V.C	Vir Clarissimus
		VE(L)	Velina
PVB	Publicus, —anus, Publilia	VEX	Vexillatio (—arii)
PVP	Pupinia	VIC	Victrix, vicus (—ani)
Q	Quaestor, Quirina, Quintus	VOL	Voltinia
R	Roma (—nus)	VOT	Voturia
ROM	Romanus, Romilia	V.P	Vir perfectissimus, votum posuit
R.P	Respublica		
S	Sacer, salve, se, semis, Sextus, Singularis, situs, solvit, stipendia, suus, etc.	V.S.L.A.	Votum solvit libens
		V.S.L.M	animo, libens merito,
		V.S.L.L.M	laetus libens merito
SAB	Sabatina	(and other variations)
SCA(P)	Scaptia	V.V	Valeria Victrix, Ulpia Victrix
SER	Sergia, Servius	VV(CC, etc.)	Viri (clarissimi)
ST	Stellatina, stipendia	Ɔ, >	Centurio (—a)
S.T.T.L	Sit tibi terra levis	∞	mille, milliaria
T	testamentum, titulus, Titus	IIII VIR	Quattuorvir
TER	Teretina	III III VIR	Sevir etc.
TES	Tesserarius	XVIR	Decemvir

INDEX

Note: References in figures alone refer to serial numbers of inscriptions (with their commentaries), while page-references are prefixed p.; EXCEPT in Index VI (Writers and Sources), where all references are to pages.

I PERSONS
having some connexion with Roman Britain

Note: Emperors are indexed under their best-known names, with Imp[erator]; other Romans under the *nomen gentilicium*. Names occurring only incidentally (e.g. of a deceased's or dedicator's company-officer or father) are not indexed unless of some interest.

II (A) ARMY UNITS IN BRITAIN

1. LEGIONS

Detachments, temporarily

II Adiutrix Pia Fidelis, 18, 28, 29, 92
II Augusta, 3, 21, 22, 74, 75, 78, 101, 117, 120, 137-9, 203, 207
VI Victrix Pia Fidelis, 74, 77, 96f, 104, 113f, 120, 140, 177, 179; B(ritannica?) 196, 211f
*VII Gemina, 98
*VIII Augusta, 98f
IX Hispana, 3, 5, 6, 19f, 33, 35, 41; p. 12; disappearance, pp. 79f
XIV Gemina, 4; Martia Victrix, 16
XX Valeria Victrix, 3, 7, 34, 74, 85f, 91f, 103, 120, 131, 159, 203
*XXII Primigenia, 98

2. ALAE

Agrippiana Miniata, 100
I Asturum, 100
II   ,,   100, 167
Augusta Gallorum, 100
Gallorum Indiana, 8
,,   Petriana, 176; Aug. M., C.R., 100; at Stanwix, p. 90
,,   Picentiana, 100
,,   Sebosiana, 95, 100, 161
Gallorum et Thracum Classiana, 100
I Pannoniorum Sabiniana, 100
I   ,,   Tampiana, 95,100
I Thracum, 95

I Tungrorum, 100
Vettonum, C.R., 80, 95, 100, 193
Augusta Vocontiorum, 100

3. AUXILIARY COHORTS

I Afrorum C.R., 100
I Alpinorum, 95
I Aquitanorum, 100, 121
II Asturum, 23, 90, 100; Sev. Alex., 205
I Baetasiorum, 95, 100; pp. 160f
I Batavorum, 100, 106, 152; Antoniniana, 153; 158
III Bracaraugustanorum, 30, 95, 100
IV Breucorum, 100
I Celtiberorum, 100
I Cornoviorum, p. 34
I Cugernorum, 95; Ulpia C.R., 100
I Aelia Dacorum, 202; Tetriciana, 210; Probiana, 215
I Delmatarum, 100
II   ,,   100
IV   ,,   95, 100, 115
I Frisiavonum, 100
II Gallorum, 100
IV   ,,   100; p. 125
V   ,,   100, 168
I Nervia Germanorum M. Eq., 100, 123
I Hamiorum Sagittariorum, 100, 128
I Hispanorum, 37, 95, 100 (? same as following)
I Hispanorum Eq., 88f; Aelia M. Eq. 203
I Lingonum Eq., 100, 118
II   ,,   Eq., 100
III   ,,   100
IV   ,,   95, 100

III   GODS AND CULTS

IV   PEOPLES AND PLACES
of Roman Britain

Note: A number after an ANCIENT name signifies that the name occurs in that inscription. Inscriptions found at a place are recorded under the MODERN name.

V   SUBJECT-INDEX

VI WRITERS AND SOURCES

(see also Note on Books)

N.B.: References are to PAGES